The Way We Are

Also by Margaret Visser

Much Depends on Dinner
The Rituals of Dinner

MARGARET VISSER

The Way We Are

A Saturday Night Book
HarperCollins*PublishersLtd*

All the pieces in this collection were previously published in
Saturday Night with the exception of "Blush, Cringe, Fidget"
which first appeared in *That Reminds Me...Canada's Authors Relive
Their Most Embarassing Moments*, Martha Kurc, ed. Stoddart, 1990.

First Edition

Canadian Cataloguing in Publication Data

Visser, Margaret, 1940-
The way we are

"A Saturday night book".
Includes index and bibliographical references.
ISBN 0-00-255419-4

I. Title.

AC8.V57 1994   081   C94-930700-9

94 95 96 97 98 99 ❖ EB 10 9 8 7 6 5 4 3 2

Printed and bound in the United States

For my sister Joan
and in memory of Tony Vorkink (1921–1994)

οἴδαμεν ὅτι ἐὰν φανερωθῇ ὅμοιοι αὐτῷ ἐσόμεθα,
ὅτι ὀψόμεθα αὐτὸν καθώς ἐστιν.

CONTENTS

FOREWORD . . . .*xi*

ACKNOWLEDGMENTS . . . .*xv*

INTRODUCTION: YES, BUT WHAT DOES IT MEAN? . . . .*xvii*

HEAVENLY HOSTESSES 1

INITIATIONS 6

AWFUL OFFAL 11

SUNSTRUCK 16

CONSPICUOUS COMPETENCE 21

TALKING TURKEY 26

NO, VIRGINIA 32

HIGH HEELS 37

BAKED BEANS: AN APOTHEOSIS 42

IN FLAGRANTE DELICTO 47

TIPS OF THE SLONGUE 52

GREETINGS 57

BEARDS 62

AVOCADOS 67

TIPPING 72

VACATIONS 77

ENGLISH SPELLING; OR WOULD YOU LIKE TO BE
    PHTHEIGHCHOUND FOR A GHOTI? 82

UMBRELLAS 87

PARADES: TAKING OVER THE STREET 93

BLUSH, CRINGE, FIDGET 98

BELLS 107

THE FEBRUARY FEAST 112

CAVIAR 117

THE PROFESSIONALS 122

THE LEFT HAND 127

WEDDING CAKE 132

TAKING A SHOWER 137

CROSSWORD PUZZLES 142

SITTING PRETTY 147

GLOVES 152

THE FIREPLACE 157

GREAT EXPECTORATIONS 162

WIGS 167

KNITTING 172

SOUR GRAPES 177

SWIMSUITS 182

MENUS 187

WEARING BLUE..192

UNCIVILIZED TO CONTEMPLATE 197

SANTA CLAUS'S SIGNIFICANT OTHER 202

STRIPES 207

THE EASTER BUNNY 212

"I MEAN, YOU KNOW, LIKE..." 217

VINEGAR AND THE SEARCH FOR SOUR 222

MAHOGANY 227

THE JOY OF JELLY 232

SYNAESTHESIA 237

RUNS, WRINKLES, SEAMS, AND SNAGS 242

CHRISTMAS PUDDING 247

HEARTS 252

FASTING 257

THE NEW ICE AGE 262

BRIGHT-EYED, BUSHY-TAILED, SERVES SIX 267

TAP-DANCING 272

BROAD BEANS 277

CHEWING GUM 282

I'LL NEVER FORGET WHATSHISNAME 287

SEEING RED 292

PAYING ATTENTION TO SNOW 297

SOUP OF THE EVENING, BEAUTIFUL SOUP 302

INDEX 307

FOREWORD

visor *or* **vizor** ('vaizə) *n.* **1.** a piece of armour fixed or hinged to the helmet to protect the face and furnished with slits for the eyes. **2.** another name for **peak** (on a cap). **3.** a small movable screen used as protection against glare from the sun. [C14: from Anglo-French *viser*, from Old French *visière*, from *vis* face; see VISAGE]—**'visored** *or* **'vizored** *adj.*—**visorless** or **vizorless** *adj.*

visserism ('visərizəm) *n.* **1.** a concise socio-anthropological insight arrived at by comparing current human behaviour with various alternative models, e.g., classical Graeco-Roman, Martian, etc. **2.** an entertainment in which points are made by identifying and skewering absurdities. **3.** any observation, esp. on contemporary manners, that provokes shocked laughter; a sly dig. **4.** *Archaic* or *literary.* the doctrine that all scholarship, e.g., food chemistry, etymology, particle physics, etc., exists to prove that life is rich, funny, and meaningful. [C20: from Anglo–South African–French *visser* to secure firmly or to screw in]—**visseriana** *noun*—**vissered** *adj.*—**visseral** *adj.*

vista ('vistə) *n.* **1.** a view, esp. through a long narrow avenue of trees, buildings, etc., or such a passage or avenue itself; prospect: a *vista of arches.* **2.** a comprehensive mental view of a distant time or a lengthy series of events: *the vista of the future* [C17: from Italian: a view from *vedere* to see, from Latin *videre*]—**vistaed** *adj.*—**vistaless** *adj.*

*   *   *

If "visserism" has not yet taken its rightful place in the dictionary, it is only because lexicographers are, as usual, slow to recognize the imperatives of everyday speech. At *Saturday Night* magazine, we can't claim to have coined the word (there are earlier citations in the archives of CBC's "Morningside," in the literature of gastronomy, and in the records of the Classics Department at the University of Toronto), but it has certainly become indispensable around our offices. For example: "There's a topic ripe for visserism." Or: "You should be vissered for that." And: "Could he make it more visseral?" We've been saying things like that for the past six years.

It was in May 1988 that Margaret Visser's unique column, "The Way We Are," started to adorn the pages of

Saturday Night. It was quickly evident to our readers that here was not just a piquant writer but a genuinely original thinker, someone with her own slant on the world around us. That's not surprising if you know her. Her great trick is to regard everything, absolutely *everything* on which her attention alights, as exotic.

The typical experience in reading a Visser column is to start off from a comfy, well-bolstered position—a nice tan makes us look healthier, for example, or Valentine's Day cards are tacky—and then, before we even have our seatbelts fastened, find ourselves whisked away in a series of brisk paragraphs through historical contexts and cultural cross-references to a destination that is neither comfy nor commonplace.

I will never forget the morning Margaret Visser's column on Santa Claus turned up on my desk in advance of a Christmas issue. "Santa Claus!" I groaned. "What in heaven's name is there left to say—one way or another—about Santa Claus?" By the time I got to the end of the column I was sweating. *A sex symbol? A spermatic journey down the shaft of a fireplace chimney? Our Santa Claus?* Ever since, I have been conscious of the impulse to distract the eyes of my impressionable children from their iconography of Jolly Old St Nick. It just doesn't seem decent anymore.

It has been much the same with her columns on high heels, broad beans, bathing suits, and the never-before-imagined possibilities offered by umbrellas. Margaret Visser has found gold in jelly, knitting, kissing, restaurant menus, stripes, the taste of sour, our failure to remember people's names—all the familiar bric-à-brac of our daily lives. But far more important than merely pinpointing the curiosities with which we surround ourselves, she has always found a way to relate to our queer behaviours and assumptions to our shared humanity. Margaret Visser is no cool, detatched observer, but a warm and gleeful participant .

I once found myself on a subway train in Toronto sitting beside a younger reader of *Saturday Night* (our range is between ten and ninety-five) who was flipping through the pages. She was just browsing, looking at the pictures in the longer features and spending altogether too much time on the advertisement for Bermuda. (It was in the middle of winter.) Then, briefly, she took in Margaret Visser's column, flipped a few more pages and then turned back to the column. In this issue, it was on the history and moral significance of blue jeans. The reader herself was wearing blue jeans. At one point while she was into the thick of the column, she actually pinched the fabric of her own clothing to get a tactile fix on its texture. At the end, she let out a little "Hmmm."

More "hmmms" have been uttered at the end of a Visser column, I suspect, than after anything else published in the magazine. They are provoked by her very visserism. Or, to be precise, they are properly called visseral "hmmms."

JOHN FRASER
Editor
Saturday Night
March 1994

ACKNOWLEDGMENTS

*T*hanks are due to many of my friends and acquaintances, who have suggested ideas, commented, criticized, and pointed out new developments I had missed. I have received constant support and inspiration from all of the members of my family. It was Nancy Colbert's idea that I should write these pieces (complete with bibliographies) as the chapters of a book. John Fraser, Editor of *Saturday Night*, commissioned me to write them for the magazine, and let me go on doing so for six years, even though they are none of them "topical." He also assigned to Barbara Moon the task of editing my work. Barbara is the best editor I have ever even heard of—tough, gracious, rigorous, insightful, lover both of structure and of detail. In ancient Rome she would have been deified as The Writer's Good Fortune.

YES, BUT WHAT DOES
IT MEAN?

*F*resh off the boat from England in August 1964, we
went into our first North American restaurant and
ordered a hamburger. We had planned this event in
advance—it was to be our first direct contact with the
reality behind images we had known through movies,
through television, through novels, through myth and fantasy, desire and suspicion and dread. We sat at a chrome-
legged table with a red vinyl top, next to a smeary window.
The waiter had come and gone, and had understood every
word we said. It was very hot; enormous cars drifted past in
the street. So far, so good. We could handle this. We were
not surprised to be given glasses of water with ice in them,
almost as soon as we sat down. We were delighted; this was

what we had been told would happen in New York, and it had happened.

The hamburger came, and with it a plastic squeeze bottle full of tomato ketchup. Less delightful, but also to be expected. I decided I would prefer mustard, and asked for some. About a minute later, the air moved slightly near my cheek, and there was a light thump as a packet of mustard hit the tabletop. After a moment's panic I turned, but the waiter was already gone, out of our ambit. The mustard lay, yellow in its transparent covering, on the table between us. It was an individual serving, just for me and not for Colin, who had not asked for any. The packet was soft and cool; the mustard was ready mixed. You were expected to tear the packet open and squeeze the mustard out with your fingers—but I could not bring myself to do that yet. We sat and looked at the mustard missile, and knew that we had reached a foreign place, an unpredictable and infinitely weird environment, which we had not come from, and into which we would slot ourselves only eventually and with the utmost difficulty. That packet of mustard was my introduction to North America.

I have been trying to understand what we participate in and what is going on around us ever since. This book represents my efforts, and the endless entertainment I have derived from them. I find, after thirty years of this, that I have fiercely guarded my original puzzled, anxious state, for it sharpens my vision and never lets my curiosity relax. I have also kept trying to understand things (like mustard packets) and behaviour (like flinging the mustard down and hurrying on), because I have found that specificities reveal principles: by focusing on small, humble, taken-for-granted objects and demeanours you can tease out of them philosophies, choices, prejudices, causes, contradictions, tragedies, absurdities. I refuse to accept the ordinary as dull: common things—it stands to reason—are the most important things, the ones with history and politics and meaning, the ones with clout.

In our "consumer" culture, we are constantly confronted with crowds of objects and with changing fashions in behaviour. The simultaneity and repetitiousness of the bombardment, the multiplicity of the things and the speed with which they reach their targets, serve to make them inscrutable to us, and exhausting in their apparent self-sufficiency and dynamism. Finally they can come to seem meaningless, and boring. But they are *there*, and they keep on requiring us to negotiate with them, even if only to find a way to keep out of their reach. My project is to grab some of them as they hurtle by. I seize one of them at a time, hold it still, and look at it closely to see where it comes from and what it might be hiding. It is important to know how we are all implicated in the existence of these culturally resonant objects, and in their form.

Because I have to catch them on the wing, as it were, when and as they occur, I have decided to present them in this book the way I found them: one by one, in *their* order—the order in which they struck me. I have also kept the chapters short, firstly because that was how I was ordered to write them; and secondly because I realized that indeed the requirement in itself, together with the speed, numbers, and variety it entailed, supplies some dramatic congruence with most people's feelings as they live their modern lives.

This higgledy-pigglediness does not mean that things are random. Not ordinary things, at any rate. For "ordinary" things are what we all know, in common. They express consensual order—what we, as a society, accept and demand and think. They can also reveal to us what we believe but never say: they can show us something of the underlying structure of social reality. If we don't take care to look at the things we take "for granted" or as "given," and try to understand them, their very ordinariness will blinker us, will start to order us around.

This book considers what our society loathes (offal, for instance, or too much facial expression), in order to ask what exactly is going on when we loathe these things. It looks for the clues to historical and social change that can be gleaned from the general adoption by our society of such things as dining-room tables, vacations, jello, or taking a shower. It is worth remembering that we once did very well without them, and had to be persuaded and then trained to accept them. The long struggle of women to be treated decently, and some recent victories in the battle, can be charted through the history of flight attendants, valentine cards, and high-heeled shoes. Ancient mythologies about women remain incorporated in Christmas trees and fireplaces.

Then there are places and stuffs set apart for key roles, for special uses and occasions, or as signs of status—take caviar, mahogany, chewing gum, boxes of chocolates, or city parks. It is also startling, as well as comforting, to realize that our society is as picturesque as any other. We have our initiations and purifications, our symbolic colours, taboo animals, and priestly professionals complete with rituals and robes. Clues can be found to our culture's presuppositions in such things as its rejection of slime, or its decision to admire the casual, the thin, and the mobile; or the suspicion with which it regards emotional intensity. Politeness is always a social lubricant, and is therefore very revealing about what it lubricates: if we look closely enough, it is possible to discern the complex need that resulted in rituals and customs such as routine kissing, sitting correctly, shaking hands, using circumlocutions, and being embarrassed in the appropriate manner and at the appropriate time.

Ideas come from the human mind, and are therefore understandable; their expression enables other people to take them in, get their minds round them, and then judge whether or not they are true. But *things* can strictly speaking never be understood: they cannot enter the mind except through the mediation of perception, attention, and thought. They are, however, *used* by the mind, played with, researched, probed by means of all the disciplines we have built up out of ideas: art, theology, philosophy, history, science, anthropology, psychology, and the rest. But we shall never comprehend (literally "altogether seize" with our minds) a thing. Things, in this sense, are ungraspable, and therefore infinitely questionable. *The Way We Are* questions the things our society uses, in order to bring not them but ourselves, the users, more sharply into focus.

HEAVENLY HOSTESSES

*T*here is an ancient insistence in our culture that women ought to be pure, and that this involves *not moving around.* Women stay home; they are there for roving males to return to. Mobility in women is therefore disconcerting and probably expressive of promiscuity. This bias is only one of the many difficulties which have bedevilled airline flight attendants throughout their short but variegated history.

Male couriers, literally "runners"—women were at first unthinkable in this role—first accompanied pilots when passengers became common in the air. Paying travellers in the 1920s had to be both rich and adventurous; there were trains and ships for the fainter-hearted. Being venturesome did not, however, preclude a need to be looked after by underlings: cosseted, comforted, fed.

Couriers helped people on with mufflers, foot-warmers, and overcoats (early planes were glacial), plugged ears with cotton batting, provided brown paper bags when needed, opened windows in flight, and then closed them on landing so that flying mud from a wet field would not enter the cabin. Passengers sat in cushioned wicker chairs, around tables set with linen cloths, china, silver cutlery, potted plants, and vases of cut flowers. As more space was provided, tables were placed along the windows as in a railway dining car. Conversation was limited to short cries and written notes, since the noise was tremendous. Mishaps with the crockery must have been frequent, because the vibration shook chairs across the floor and worked eyeglasses invariably down people's noses.

Meals were served, cold but magnificent and with many courses, by men in white jackets and gloves. When night flights began there were foldout beds with sheets, pillows, and blankets, and stewards woke passengers with china cups of tea. Bowls of soup as well as coffee and tea could be heated on a stove in the rear of the aircraft. This serving of meals and tea had changed the courier's name: he was now a steward, on an analogy with ocean liner staff. He was always male and white, in North America as well as in Europe.

In May 1930, the first six women began to serve customers on aircraft. It was an American idea, daring and brilliant. Who cared if women got mobile? Some could surely be found who were able to withstand the dangers and fight off the innuendoes of night stopovers, long distances away from home, and constant movement. There were other, more immediately convenient, myths to hand.

These women were welcoming *hostesses* (the new name doubtless helped), every one a registered nurse, capable, motherly, and understanding. They wore green suits on the ground but white nurses' attire, with capes and caps, on board. Their job was to comfort passengers, and give a good example by not, though women, showing fear.

They were strong too, even though they were unacceptable unless under 5 ft. 4 in. in height and weighing less than 120 lb. They carried luggage on board and unloaded the aircraft again at the end of the journey. They cleaned messes, dusted the plane inside and out, helped fuel it and mend punctures, and might even assist the pilot to push it into the hangar. They held passengers' hands going up and down steps, hovered over the bilious, prevented visitors to the washroom from opening the exit door by mistake, and pointed out the places of interest passing below. If all seats were full the hostess would sit on the mailbag at the back of the plane.

Gradually, more and more women were accepted for work on aircraft both within the U.S. and elsewhere, but they really only "arrived" after the War. And immediately their job took on, along with nursing and waitressing, the third aspect: stewardesses were to be selected for looks. Besides having to be white, under twenty-five, and certifiably unmarried, they had to undergo cosmetic training, hairstyling, and lessons in how to charm male passengers. Rules for achieving this demanded relentless smiling and mandatory "eye contact," as well as cunning methods of walking and climbing steps.

The myth of the Swinging Stewardesses took off, at once empowered by ancient suspicions surrounding "unbridled mobility," especially in women. One airline advertised, "I'm Cheryl—Fly Me." Braniff International "ended the plain plane" in 1966, offering "stews" who made several flashy costume changes en route, ending with hot pants. Travellers with another airline were treated to in-flight announcements set to a perky jingle and sung by the stewardesses. A rioting planeload of drunken male football fans once forced the women to take refuge in the cockpit while the pilots made an unscheduled landing.

The trend was finally quashed, but only in the feminist seventies, after innumerable scandals and complaints, and a series of court rulings. Hostesses were eventually permitted to marry and have children if they chose; they could no longer be dismissed because of age; and the profession was at last opened to blacks. The change of image brought about a new official name, "flight attendants": long, colourless yet slickly modern, and unisex. For by 1972, prestige as well as respectability having been restored, males were re-entering the field.

Bibliography

Kenneth Hudson and Julian Pettifer, *Diamonds in the Sky: A Social History of Air Travel*. London: Bodley Head, 1979.

Paula Kane and Christopher Chandler, *Sex Objects in the Sky*. Chicago: Follett, 1974.

Elizabeth R. Moles and Norman L. Friedman, "The Airline Hostess: Realities of an Occupation with a Popular Cultural Image," *Journal of Popular Culture* 7 (1973) 305–13.

Emily Post, *Etiquette*. Compare the 1937 edition, "Travel by Air," p. 828, and the 1950 edition, "Special Aspects of Air Travel" and "The Young Girl Traveling Alone," pp. 602–3. New York: Funk and Wagnall.

Jean-Pierre Vernant, "Hestia—Hermès: sur l'expression religieuse de l'espace et du mouvement chez les Grecs," in *Mythe et pensée chez les Grecs*, tome I, pp. 124–70. Paris: Maspéro, 1974.

INITIATIONS

*F*luid and mobile societies avoid initiations—so the anthropological wisdom goes. This is said partly in order to explain, of course, why our own society (the society of the anthropologists) seems so nonchalantly to do without initiations. Not for us the terror of living alone for months in the bush, of being daubed in white paint and chanted over, of mutilations of the sexual organs, of leaping over thornbushes or having to see visions in order to ready ourselves for a new role in the next inexorable stage of life.

We keep moving, through the doors which our culture opens so readily (or so its myth proclaims) from status to status, with hardly a pause to notice the thresholds *en passant*. It's as much as we can do to move fast enough: no need, no *time* for initiations, thank you very much.

Yet initiations do survive among us—though often

disguised by what the French call *méconnaissance*: our own decision usually not to notice they are occurring, or what they really mean. Openly recognized initiations take place mainly in the domain of religion. Ceremonies like Baptism, Bar Mitzvah, and First Communion all involve complex and solemn drama; they mark clear entrances into new stages of life, knowledge, and commitment.

Weddings are initiatory ceremonies in all cultures; even in our own the traditional elements remain. Examples include the wearing of extraordinary clothes expressing purity and fertility; the swearing of oaths administered by official Elders; acceptance of rings as symbols of irrevocability; the flinging of many small objects at the newly professed; a momentous "honeymoon" journey, and so on.

People who go through initiations are transformed thereby: they leave a lower status for a higher. They learn a new thing, usually how to play a new role, and having passed through the ordeal (initiations are often deliberately set up as ordeals) there is no going back. One dresses differently during the ritual, and may receive the right to wear picturesque robes thereafter. Very often one is given a new name or title; in many societies the initiate's body itself is symbolically marked, sometimes for life.

An important rule is that the harder the initiation is to achieve, the stronger the solidarity of the group into which the candidate is admitted. This may be one reason why initiations are "played down" among us: we discourage the formation of strongly committed groups in our society.

Take, for example, the suspiciously regarded group solidarity of our four great professions (some would call them the *only* professions): clergy, doctors, lawyers, and university professors. All these brotherhoods demand formidable ritual initiations. The rites usually begin with a sending of candidates away from home. There may follow a cruel hazing procedure by the Seniors (previously initiated) of the group.

Novices endure long years of seclusion from the public, all kinds of demeaning but ineluctable tasks, instruction in arcana by powerful older members, and a series of punishing examinations. To make it into the exclusive upper stratum, you have not only to suffer but to be *seen* to be suffering by your future peers, just as they themselves suffered once. Survivors are finally decorated with titles, uniforms, certificates, and other symbolic regalia.

Submission is the essence of initiation: submission above all to the Elders. Society is experienced as almost omnipotent, and immutable: a diagram to which the changing individual must conform, cutting and stretching himself or herself where necessary.

Acquiring a taste for initially unpleasant or unhealthy food and drink is a mild modern version of initiation. With grim determination we swallow bitter beer till we finally like it and "join the men." Coffee and tea are not allowed to children (a useful prohibition for parents who wish to have a few peaceful interludes in the day for themselves and their friends)—until the day the children are old enough to "take it," and so be admitted to a new age set.

First nylon stockings and first lipstick are girls' initiation rites, as can be a boy's first haircut at the barber shop with Dad. It was once traditional for the agonies of learning to smoke to be voluntarily undergone as a sign of entry to adolescence. Suntanning, that expensive and uncomfortable changing of one's colour and markings, was undergone in order to demonstrate the achievement of sufficient money and modernity, and also a laudable submission to social conventions regarding youth, health, and beauty.

How difficult and annoying it now is for people to give up their initiatory status, suddenly being exhorted—by society itself!—to forgo cancerous sunbathing, disgusting and irresponsible smoking, and stupidly hectic coffee: we tried so hard and so obediently to achieve the habits in the first place. Thinness remains a *sine qua non*, however, and heaven knows that that stipulation is difficult, costly, and time-consuming enough to cut our psyches as well as our figures down to size. The priesthood administering this particular rite has it made, because thinness is a multivalent initiation, requiring endless efforts at renewal; in the end, traditional, once-in-a-lifetime ritual tattoos and scarification were probably kinder.

Bibliography

Mircea Eliade, *Rites and Symbols of Initiation*. Trans. W.R. Trask. New York: Harper Torchbooks, 1958.

Les Rites d'initiation. Actes du Colloque de Liège et de Louvain-la-neuve, 20–21 novembre 1984, ed. J. Ries and H. Limet. Louvain-la-neuve: Centre d'histoire des religions, 1986.

Victor Turner, *The Ritual Process*. Chicago: Aldine, 1969.

Arnold Van Gennep, *Les Rites de passage*. Paris: E. Nourry, 1909.

AWFUL OFFAL

$\mathcal{S}$ ylvia Plath is said to have made the following pronouncement when still an infant:

Liver, liver
Makes me shiver.

It was an impressive poetic début.

Fifty-five years later, the very thought of liver is still upsetting for most North Americans. Converts to the recent gourmet revolution, it is true, now venture where it was once thought only "ethnic" people would care to go. They find themselves coping not only with liver (which is actually the least offensive of innards to mainstream North Americans) but also with tripe, brains, hearts, trotters, tails, tongues, sweetbreads, and kidneys—every one of them the object, in various traditions, of loving culinary attention.

Yet contemporary gourmets, even French ones, seem to pass over in silence some of the anatomical parts our own forefathers relished, such as palates, spleens, cockscombs, and snouts. Stuffed calves' eyes *au gratin* and braised eyes *sauce vinaigre* were greatly extolled in eighteenth-century France. One will still find people who like ears and testicles.

The ancient Greeks valued the *splanchna,* or viscera, above all other animal parts, with the exception perhaps of the fat. When you sacrificed an ox you split it up the middle, plunged your hands in, and at once snatched up and examined the liver. Deep inside the beast, it infallibly reflected reality. Did it faultlessly shine? What did its lobes, its portal-vein and gall-sac portend?

Next, the *splanchna* were cut up and speared as shish kebabs, which an élite inner circle of attendants was allowed to eat immediately. The ordinary meat was shared out later to *hoi polloi.* There is relatively little in any animal of what North Americans call "organ meats," so that getting some was for the few; it was a mark of great prestige.

The distinction between "meat" and "innards" has survived in traditional North American thought patterns, but the values are reversed. Organs are revolting for being smooth, wobbly, and shiny when raw, and still slithery or dark and firm-textured cooked. Notwithstanding Leopold Bloom's love of "a fine tang of faintly scented urine" in kidneys, most of us find any hint of excretory functions impossible to contemplate with pleasure.

All the innards tend to be lumped together in our speech, as we delicately (or with disgust) overlook their differences and separateness. The British call them *offal* (they *fall off* in the butchering). The word confirms the worst suspicions of North Americans: *offal* tends for them to mean simply "garbage." And indeed the original meaning of "garbage" was "offal, especially the entrails."

"Variety meats" is a name sometimes given to viscera by those trying to get us to buy them: the suggestion is that they lend variety to our menu. But also, *they are themselves various*, and herein lies a problem. Each of the viscera has its own peculiar texture and shape, and every organ has a function that is all too familiar. Kidneys, hearts, or tripe distressingly maintain their identities, even after chopping and under sauce.

A slice of beef might be known to come, say, from the leg, but we think of it as beef and not as a piece of leg. Anyway, legs are mechanical things—not nearly so closely linked with a creature's essential character as are its "vital organs." Our language traditionally equates these with personal courage: a person *of kidney*, who has *guts* or shows *pluck*, is brave, while a coward can be called *lily-livered*.

"Offal" must be eaten fresh: it keeps far less satisfactorily than "meat," and this must be one reason why it has come to fit our cultural expectations so imperfectly. Innards seem to have become devalued in England in about 1800, when slaughterhouses were giving them away to the poor for immediate consumption. Their collective name was *numbles, umbles* in some dialects. *Umble* eventually seemed to be *h*-less for *humble*, so that a person who "ate humble pie" joined the ranks of those whose status was low.

The new predilection for gourmet foods, which are often foreign in origin, is now changing the value system once again. Food that is thought of as sophisticated and prestigious often looks and tastes rather odd to begin with. (It also repels the naive majority, those who have not learned to confront it.) And if such a bizarre notion as eating neck-glands in sauce comes garnished with French culinary approval, then neck-glands (known euphemistically to us as *sweetbreads*) become suddenly very expensive, where once they were irritably discarded.

But eyes—no. We still need a lot of persuading before we will accept eyes. Not even the French recommend eyes any more.

Bibliography

Guy Berthiaume, *Les rôles du mageiros. Etude sur la boucherie, la cuisine et le sacrifice dans la Grèce ancienne.* Montréal: Presses de l'Université, 1982.

Marcel Detienne and Jean-Pierre Vernant, *La cuisine du sacrifice en pays grec.* Paris: Gallimard, 1979.

Jean-Louis Durand and Annie Schnapp, "Boucherie sacrificielle et chasses initiatiques," in C. Bérard et al., eds., *La cité des images.* Paris: Fernand Nathan, 1984, pp. 49–54.

James Joyce, *Ulysses.* Episode 4 (Calypso), p. 106. New York and London: Garland Publishing, 1984 (originally published 1922).

Stephen Mennell, *All Manners of Food.* Oxford: Basil Blackwell, 1985, pp. 310–16.

William Shakespeare, *Macbeth.* Act V, scene iii, l. 15.

SUNSTRUCK

*F*or two hundred years, from the 1730s to the 1920s, if you were rich and English, and wished to take a dip in the sea, you used a bathing-machine. This was a covered wooden wagon with steps leading up to a door at the back. A horse and driver drew this cabin on wheels, with the bathers inside, into the sea. The horse then turned the whole thing round and waited, facing the beach, for the swimming session to end.

Many bathing-machines were provided with canvas awnings which were let down to the water's surface. The bathers went down the steps and into the water in darkness, splashed about, and returned to the cabin to dress. The "machine" protected them from the gaze of spectators, and from the sun. Men and women bathed separately; men usually bathed naked, and women wore long dresses which were modest when dry.

On the beach itself, people sat hatted, corseted, with parasols and boots, and with clothing covering them from their necks to their ankles. Lotion was applied to any exposed flesh, to prevent it from becoming brown. If you were rich enough to be able to afford the brilliantly modern and medicinal rites of sea-bathing, you had not the slightest wish to find yourself back in Society with tanned surfaces showing.

For centuries a brown skin had been the mark of a rustic, one who was compelled to work and who therefore could not avoid the sun. The nobility were distinguished by white skin, and by hands so soft they could never be accused of having toiled.

In classical Greece and Rome, the difference between white and tanned skin had been a sexual convention. Men were brown and women white, because women's place was at home indoors, while men ranged abroad and concerned themselves with such pursuits as farming, sailing, politics, and war.

The difference in flesh-tones between the sexes had a further, deliciously perverse excitement. Women, in the cosmological system of opposites that obtained in Greece and Rome, were classed as dark, while men were light. Earth was dark, cold, and female, the sun hot, light, and male, and so forth. How thrilling then that men, out in the sun, were dark, whereas women, within the darkened house, had light skin.

In 1902, the hero of André Gide's novel *L'Immoraliste* took off his clothes and lay down in the sun. This was the first sunbathing scene in French literature; real-life French people were not to start voluntarily browning themselves for another twenty-five years.

Before they did so, a group of rich artists and foreigners, many of them Americans, had begun to stay in the south of France for the summer, and not (as aristocrats had been doing for a century) during the winter. Gerald and Sara Murphy, Scott Fitzgerald, Aldous Huxley, and others like them had decided to go south and go brown. They were the new trend-setters. When paid holidays arrived as a social reality, the general race to the beaches began.

It was no longer infra dig to be brown. On the contrary: for some time it had been the *workers* who were white, toiling in factories and offices. The rich and adventurous could escape from the cities (it took a lot of time away from working and a great deal of expense to get to the Riviera) and obtain for themselves strong physiques and suntans. Paleness now denoted the financially unendowed, the unhealthy, and those definitely "left behind."

As soon as there were paid vacations and cheap transport to the sun, everybody rushed to enjoy the fun and the fresh air. You flung off your clothes, lay luxuriously down, and began to feel free. Soon everybody was doing it; you had to be there too, or miss out socially. A day at the seaside, a chance to lie about and burn your skin between dips in the cooling water came to seem a thing universally and invariably to be longed for. You could not really be a happy person unless you regularly experienced it. Sunbathing was a form of initiation, a pseudo-religious rite that facilitated social acceptance. And every annual recreation meant new body-markings, which were brought home as a kind of holiday souvenir.

Patterning one's skin has always been sexually provocative and exciting; being perfectly tanned was one way to be perceived as sexually alert, and probably successful as well. The ritual—of semi-sacred places, ointments, and postures, the gathering in crowds, the special clothing, and the mask-like sunglasses—added to the mysterious delight of it all.

The suntanning craze has been a phenomenon unparalleled in human history. It reached its peak in the 1970s, but is now in full retreat. Skin cancer and premature aging of the skin are mentioned discouragingly often. People have found that there are more ways than lying on beaches to achieve happiness; pale skins have begun to look less unappetizing than they once did. Indeed, people with skins burned a deliberate, beach-earned bronze are beginning to look just plain ignorant. A suntan, in any case, has become much too easy to obtain for it to be satisfactory as a status symbol: after all, *anyone*, if they are silly enough, can get to be brown now.

Bibliography

André Gide, *L'Immoraliste*. Part I, Chapter VI. Paris: Pléi-ade, 1958 (first published 1902).

Sarah Howell, *The Seaside*. London: Cassell and Collier Macmillan, 1974.

Muriel Searle, *Bathing Machines and Bloomers*. Tunbridge Wells: Midas Books, 1977.

Giorgio Triani, *Pelle di luna, pelle di sole: nascità e storia della civiltà balneare 1700–1946*. Venice: Marsilio, 1988.

John K. Walton, *The English Seaside Resort: A Social History 1750–1914*. Leicester University Press, 1983.

James Walvin, *Beside the Seaside: A Social History of the Popular Seaside Holiday*. London: Allen Lane, 1978.

John Weightman, "The Solar Revolution: Reflections on a Theme in French Literature," *Encounter* 35 (December 1970) 9–18.

CONSPICUOUS
COMPETENCE

*I*n *The Importance of Being Earnest,* Cecily boasts that
when she sees a spade she calls it a spade. Gwendolen
crushingly responds: "I am glad to say that I have never
seen a spade. It is obvious that our social spheres have
been widely different."

Four years later, in 1899, Thorstein Veblen published
The Theory of the Leisure Class. The book elaborates upon
the idea behind Wilde's jest. In rounded, majestic sen-
tences, Veblen dissected the prestige that adhered to
wealth and privilege in the 1890s.

The rich, he said, were quite simply useless people:
never having seen a spade was precisely what gave them
their clout. The secret of their high social status was

waste—waste of money, and waste of time. They did nothing, and paid others to work instead; they spent fortunes on gambling, feasting, travelling, and dressing their wives in extravagant, work-impeding clothes. Veblen coined two phrases in his book to describe the twin and absurd buttresses of upper-class mystique—*conspicuous leisure* and *conspicuous consumption*. These soon became stock insights, and remained dear to the hearts of sociologists for over fifty years.

But it is clear now that even Veblen's views were determined by a particular place and time. The son of Norwegian immigrants to the U.S., he had been educated to loathe poor productivity. For all his iconoclastic wit, Veblen wrote in fact from deep within the North American work ethic. We can still laugh at Wilde's sally, and still profitably read Veblen, or parts of him at any rate. But something has changed. The modern snobbery system has had time to shift its ground—retaining its authority, of course.

For some time, consumption has renounced being brashly conspicuous. A torn T-shirt, holes in one's jeans, dirty sneakers, a faded fisherman's sweater have all revealed their potential for snob appeal. The rich have learned to wear rags in order outrageously to reveal their power: we have accustomed ourselves to read, as it were, through the rips. Conspicuous consumption, in certain spheres of life at least, remains *out*.

What is *in* is likely to be formidably tough denim, cutaway "muscle shirts," and very specific sporting gear: tight bicycle shorts, and bright glossy "surfing" outfits. The reigning chic suggests tremendous fitness and proficiency in those who can afford it: one might call it *conspicuous competence*. The point is that it is now not the rich but the lower ranks who are classified as, and encouraged to remain, incapable. The rich, it follows, are rich because they are *qualified*. The process of deskilling the lower classes has been proceeding, efficiently, for years.

Time was when ordinary people did the cooking, the rug-hooking, the gardening. It was they who were physically fit from manual labour, who wore strong clothes (often a peasant blue) which facilitated movement and provided the necessary pockets. Now the privileged and successful have invaded all this territory.

The "gourmet revolution" is (among other things) the "upwardly mobile" members of society annexing the culinary skills: it is harder for working-class people to find the time or the money for conspicuous creativity in the kitchen. Everything is set up to let them eat fast food, and drink what is appropriately known as "pop." A lower-class, non-ethnic North American might well feel nonplussed when confronting an eggplant. It can take many years of determination and polish before aubergines fried, roasted, coated with yoghurt, grilled, stuffed, or sliced in fans will habitually grace one's chic and competent table.

Cuisinarts, German knives, and an Italian kitchen with a plain but "professional" six-burner stove are all helpful, it is true. And the tired but rich gourmet can always split and take to a restaurant—safe, if he or she is careful, from the fast-food multitude. The gilt-edged children of the middle class must become conspicuously competent as well. They are weaned on personal computers (*such* an advantage, as the early ads in magazines for the wealthy openly reminded their readers), initiated into the exclusive games, and taught early on to wear rags with flair.

The modern "business" suit for men was an ingenious device for disguising the appalling physiques of the sedentary nineteenth-century rich. Such suits were a disadvantage to the muscular, especially when cheaply made. Now that the top people ripple with expensive health, they want "casual" or streamlined clothes, to enhance their splendidly fit forms.

Walking is generally recommended. A woman with three cars in her garage will walk miles, purely for fitness, wearing high-tech sneakers which required great erudition in the choosing, and many inconspicuous dollars to buy. She might even purchase a calibrated treadmill so that she can perform the same feat in her own home, protected from the pollution of the street. For it is not enough to own a fortune now: you must also be persuaded that you deserve it.

Bibliography

Benita Eisler, *Class Act*. New York: F. Watts, 1983.

Thorstein Veblen, *The Theory of the Leisure Class*. Boston: Houghton Mifflin, 1973 (first published 1899).

Oscar Wilde, *The Importance of Being Earnest*, in Joseph Bristow, ed., *The Importance of Being Earnest and Related Writings*. London, New York: Routledge, 1992 (first published in 1895).

TALKING TURKEY

"*R*ugose and carunculated," Audubon called its head and neck: all wrinkly and covered with flabby wattles, warts, tubercles, and bumps. The weirdest of a turkey's fifty or so caruncles is attached to its face; in the male this cone of flesh, drooping over its bill, can stretch in a trice from one to ten centimetres in length.

The whole featherless neck and head changes colour as the turkey's moods alter, from white to turquoise to blue, to pink, purple, orange, and flaming red. When the male is courting, the flat skin of his neck is red and the warty caruncles brilliant blue. The bird gobbles; he struts and puffs (the latter performance is called a *pfum*), and his tail feathers display in the manner of a peacock.

The Indians used the feathers for headdresses, arrows, and fans, or twisted them on cords and wove them into cloaks and highly efficient blankets. The male has a black bristle "beard" hanging from his chest, which was used to sprinkle water in religious ceremonies.

Columbus encountered the bird first on an island off the coast of Honduras, where the Indians served some to him roasted; at other Indian feasts the Spaniards were offered vast tamales containing a whole turkey each. The appearance of the living birds astounded, fascinated, and confused the Europeans, who ended up calling the creature *Meleagris gallopavo*: "guineafowl chickenpeacock."

The popular name varies from Indian tribe to tribe, and from country to country. The English thought the huge new chicken originated in Turkey, and the French and Italians named it "from India" (*dinde* and *gallo d'India*); the Turks themselves called it *hindi*. Persians said it was a *filmurgh* or "elephant bird," because of its size and maybe also because of the main caruncle; and the Japanese, awed perhaps by all those changing wattles, call it *shichimencho*: "seven-faced."

Turkeys are extraordinarily primitive fowl in certain respects. They seem never to think of looking down when seeking an escape route, and their eyeballs fit so tightly into their sockets that they have to turn their heads to see moving objects. A deafened female turkey, hearing no sound from her young, will take them for foreign pests and peck them to death; and a turkey with mud on its head may be murdered by its brethren for looking odd. The birds can become enraged by unusual rocks or old bones; at any unexpected noise all males and some females gobble madly. Their stupidity has become proverbial: in eighteenth-century France *dindonné* meant "duped," like English "gulled"; and calling somebody "a turkey" today is ruder still.

The position of the female's head and neck is essential in turkey mating: cocks will display before a disembodied hen's head crudely carved in wood, provided the thing is held at precisely the seductive angle. Turkeys can reproduce by parthenogenesis (eggs may hatch young without sex), which places them early on the avian evolutionary chain.

The wild turkey is almost extinct in its pure state; it is believed that nearly all those now being carefully conserved in the wild have some admixture of domestic blood. Wild turkeys roamed eastern North America in flocks of thousands when the Europeans arrived. They squatted in the trees, huge and utterly unafraid of human beings; in many Indian tribes adult men scorned to hunt them, leaving turkey-catching to children because they were such easy game.

Turkeys were shot with so much abandon by the European settlers that their numbers declined rapidly. As early as 1672, John Josselyn wondered whether wild turkeys might soon disappear forever. There was a tremendous loss of habitat, including a large-scale depletion of ginseng berries, one of the favourite foods of turkeys. Ginseng plants and roots were exported for excellent prices to the Chinese market.

Mexican Indians had domesticated the turkey in pre-Columbian times. The U.S. and Canada, however, got domestic turkeys not from Central America but from England

and France, where they were bred from birds imported from Spain. Almost as soon as they reached Europe, turkeys began to supplant peacocks, and eventually geese, as the "great birds" traditionally eaten at Christmas and other celebrations. Turkeys are impressively large and turn golden with basting; their capacious insides inspire creativity in the stuffing.

Turkey breasts were an instant favourite with American and Canadian colonists, who often dried, ground, and kneaded the powdered meat to make cheap and easy "bread." Geneticists have grossly enlarged the turkey's breast. They have also made the bird delicate, susceptible to cold and wet, almost incapable of copulating (fertilization has to be achieved with human help), and sometimes unsteady on its feet because of its bulging *embonpoint*.

The meat it offers is not only light, the most preferred, but also dark, which lends variety. Darkness in bird meat comes from the myoglobin which stores oxygen for muscles; the breasts of game birds are dark because they fly. Legs are dark in the domesticated turkey because even battery-raised birds have to stand, and so make use of the muscles in their legs.

In eighteenth-century Europe and North America, long before refrigeration and swift transport, flocks of turkeys were commonly walked a hundred miles or more to market so that they could be slaughtered when and where they were bought and eaten. From the large breeding farms in Norfolk thousands of birds crowded down the narrow roads to London during the weeks preceding Christmas.

The great black Norfolk gobblers (which the English called "bubbly-jocks") wore shoes for the journey. Their feet were dipped in thick pitch, tied up in sacking, or covered with little boots to protect them on the long noisy march south. Dark meat must definitely have predominated by the time turkeys arrived upon city dinner tables.

Bibliography

John James Audubon, *Ornithological Biography.* Vol. I, p. 17. Edinburgh: A. Black, 1831.

Sally Smith Booth, *Hung, Strung, and Potted.* New York: Potter, 1971, pp. 94–95.

E.B. Hale and M.W. Schein, "The Behaviour of Turkeys," in E.S.E. Hafez, ed., *The Behaviour of Domestic Animals.* London: Baillière, Tindall and Cox, 1962, pp. 531–64.

John Josselyn, *New England's Rarities Discovered.* 1672. Reprinted, Boston: Massachusetts Historical Society Picture Books, 1972, p. 9.

Paul Levy, *The Feast of Christmas.* London: Kyle Cathie, 1992, pp. 79–102.

Harold McGee, *On Food and Cooking.* New York: Charles Scribner's Sons, 1984, pp. 92–93.

A.W. Schorger, *The Wild Turkey: Its History and Domestication.* Norman: University of Oklahoma Press, 1966.

Judy Urquhart, *Animals on the Farm.* London and Sydney: Macdonald, 1983, pp. 160–65.

Barbara Ketcham Wheaton, *Savoring the Past: The French Kitchen and Table from 1300 to 1789.* The University of Pennsylvania Press, 1983, pp. 81–82.

NO, VIRGINIA

*T*he modern version of him first took shape in New York City in 1822. He was very small indeed at that date, an elf in fact, who fitted with ease into the narrowest chimney stack. He flew through the air in a sleigh full of toys, drawn by reindeer who could land on rooftops. His clothes, which covered him from head to foot in fur, were understandably begrimed with soot. He was a heavy smoker.

The elf grew into a giant as the years passed; he gave up his pipe and became cleaner and cleaner. He started to dress in gnomes' red outfits, gnomes' caps, and a broad leather belt and boots. He had been bearded from the start, and the fur of his coat—now a lining merely—became snow-white to match his hair. In his earlier days he used to chuckle quietly, gripping his pipe between his teeth, shaking his round belly, and presumably wheezing a bit; but later on he took to roaring with laughter—rather mirthlessly, but very loud.

There is no story at all. Just a workshop for making toys in the North Pole, a few anecdotes about one of his reindeer, and that's about it. We once heard his wife mentioned occasionally, but she has been forgotten, swallowed up (metaphorically, of course) by him; several writers for psychiatric journals say he now has markedly androgynous features.

He is not a myth (myths require stories); he is a symbol, an image, a personification. He has become a totally benevolent figure, symbolizing aspects of the season: gift-giving, lots of fun and food, and children above all. Christmas is an old feast, and vigorous, like him.

In him Christmas is opposed to New Year's. That is to say, he is for family, domesticity, and children; New Year's is for singles, and raucous parties away from home. He rewards past good behaviour (he *knows* if you've been bad, but he never takes it out on you), whereas New Year's brings sober resolutions for the future.

There is no question that he is a fertility figure—abundance, fatness, generosity, babies. (In his bad old days that partiality for babies often meant that he enjoyed eating them.) He is obviously phallic: dressed in red, coming down the chimney, and leaving a present in the stocking. Some analysts have suspected that he is, at the same time, pregnant.

His presents are for all children, but only for children. Gift-giving can often be construed as requiring some sort of return: a thing or a service of equal value to the original gift, if not something in kind. But here is an occasion for giving on one side and simple receiving on the other. Children are not bound by obligation to return anything: the giant gnome takes off too fast for any recompense. Adults simply watch and enjoy the pleasure given.

The Christmas crib has contributed other details: the old man bringing gifts to a child, coming down from heaven at night, arriving complete with animals, and so on. But the old man is also a superb business proposition, obligingly embodying everything about Christmas that is useful in a big store. Not being religious, he can cheerfully shoulder the task of encouraging and glorifying consumerism, and so allow people who are busy shopping to bypass the crib, the birth narrative, the poor, salvation, and God.

He operates, of course, hand-in-glove with parents; in fact, he would not be around without their help. It really is a lot of work keeping it all up: the children informed, their expectations built up, then gratified. Why do we do it?

Well, for one thing our parents did it to us, and we remember. Other parents are doing it for their children, and our child must not be left out. And parents love it: the excitement, opening the presents, the whole atmos-phere—it enables them not only to be generous but to relive, through their children, the days long ago, before they themselves found out.

One of the things we all remember, don't we, is the day we found out. Someone told us; we overheard; we sudden-ly realized. We did our best not to show disappointment, of course—we might even have pretended for a while that we didn't know, for the sake of younger siblings, or even to keep our parents happy. This was growing up; we had to take it "like a man," show that we were not really surprised, that we didn't especially care.

And this is, of course, why he's there: set up for children to see through, when they are ready. He is an ingenious initiation device, whose vanishing means that the line between innocence and "the age of reason" has been crossed. In this rite of passage there is no revelation, only demystification.

No guide is provided for the initiate either: she is left to find out the truth, *for herself*. All of a sudden she learns many things: that parents are *not* always what they seem, that she should greet information with caution at all times, and never again expect kindness just because she exists.

Bibliography

Anon., "Yes, Virginia, There is a Santa Claus." Editorial page, *New York Sun*, 24 December 1897.

James H. Barnett, *The American Christmas: A Study in National Culture*. New York: Macmillan, 1954.

Warren O. Hagstrom, "What Is the Meaning of Santa Claus?" *The American Sociologist*, November 1966, 248–52.

François André Isambert, *La Fin de l'année*. Paris: Société des amis du Centre d'études sociologiques, 1976.

Samuel L. Macey, *Patriarchs of Time*. Athens: University of Georgia Press, 1987.

Clement C. Moore, "A Night before Christmas," reprinted in Martin Ebon, *Saint Nicholas: Life and Legend*. New York: Harper and Row, 1975.

G.J. Moschetti, "The Christmas Potlatch: A Refinement on the Sociological Interpretation of Gift Exchange," *Sociological Focus* 12 (1979) 1–7.

Eric R. Wolf, "Santa Claus: Notes on a Collective Representation," in Robert A. Manners, ed., *Process and Pattern in Culture*. Chicago: Aldine, 1964, pp. 147–55.

HIGH HEELS

*I*n Alfred Hitchcock's movie *The Lady Vanishes*, a nun is shockingly revealed to be no nun. She is sitting sedately enough, but we suddenly notice, protruding from beneath her habit, a pair of high-heeled shoes. Footwear of that shape immediately signals to us that this is a woman playing the sexual game.

When clothing resembling nuns' habits was ordinary female apparel, there were no such things as heels of any sort. Heels appeared for the first time in France in the 1590s. They were quite high and worn first by men. It was soon realized that heels had their uses as stirrup-holders on riding boots. But their first purpose was to raise their owners, enable them to pose impressively, and stretch their legs so that their calf muscles bulged curvaceously out.

Women quickly took to wearing heels although their legs were hidden by voluminous skirts, and when they did hemlines rose to show off their shoes. High-heeled shoes are still meant predominantly for posing in, as Miss America does in her swimsuit. She keeps her legs together, one knee gently bent. Pictures of women in bathing suits with heeled legs astride make a more up-to-date, but not necessarily a more feminist, statement.

High heels have never been made for comfort or for ease of movement. Their first wearers spoke of themselves as "mounted" or "propped" upon them; they were strictly court wear, and constituted proof that one intended no physical exertion, and need make none.

The Chinese had long known footwear that had the same effect, with high wooden pillars under the arch of each shoe, so that wearers required one or even two servants to help them totter along. Women had their feet deformed, by binding, into tiny, almost useless fists, which were shod in embroidered bootees: men got out of the thought of these an unconscionable thrill.

The European versions of stilt-shoes were Venetian chopines, which grew in height to twenty inches and more. The shoes attached to these pedestals sloped slightly towards the toe, and this is believed to be one origin of the heel. The other was the thoroughly mundane and practical patten or wooden clog, which raised the whole foot and was slipped over shoes to protect them from mud and water in the street.

High heels seem to have derived from an attempt to lighten raised shoes, by first creating an arch, then letting the toe down to the ground. The metatarsi of the foot (the long bones that end in toes) would remain bent, and bear the weight of the downward thrust.

And immediately the comforts of left and right shoes ceased to exist. "Straights," or both shoes made exactly alike, arrived with heels; people had to swap their left and right shoes every day, to keep them in shape. Fitted lefts and rights returned only when fashion dispensed with heels—until the pantograph changed shoemaking technology in the nineteenth century and made heeled lefts and rights feasible.

High heels became distinctively female dress during the eighteenth century: men heartily approved. "Heels" cause a woman's bottom to undulate twice as much as flat shoes permit; they pleasingly hobble the female and give the male a protective function; they add curve to the leg by shortening the heel cords and raising calf muscles. Sling-back shoes and curving heels help draw attention to the *back* of a woman: it is the ancient device of rewarding the turning of a male's head. Tall cones or "stiletto" heels are aggressive yet incapacitating, like long fingernails.

There has always been a preference for tiny feet in women: even prehistoric Venuses' legs tend to taper to a point. This might be because animals, especially stream-lined ones like cats, dogs, and horses, have short feet or hooves. High heels and skimpy shoes reduce feet and lengthen legs; they emphasize the animal in woman. Also—and this is important sexually—stretched legs show that she is taut and *trying*.

Pointed toes redouble the discomfort factor, and cut feet smaller still. Points plus heels aim at lightness, emphasizing the "animal" message—but also stylizing it. They give women an ethereal aspect by raising them from the earth and from common sense.

After the French Revolution the idea of using high heels to advertise status became embarrassing, and women and men went immediately into flats (very insubstantial ones if you were upper class). Men soon regained a small heel to secure the straps under their feet that held their trouserlegs tight. It was at this very date that ballerinas, heelless in ordinary life, took to dancing on points.

Fashion historians tell us that women don strong shoes, low heels, and round toes whenever society feels threatened and politics uncertain. They are a sure sign that people—men as well as women—are worried, and gearing up for a fight.

Bibliography

Lincoln Kirstein, *Movement and Metaphor: Four Centuries of Ballet.* New York: Praeger, 1970.

Irvana Malabarba, *Signori, le scarpe!* Milan: Idealibri, 1985.

June Swann, *Shoes.* London: B.T. Batsford, 1982.

Eunice Wilson, *A History of Shoe Fashions.* London: Pittman, 1969.

BAKED BEANS: AN
APOTHEOSIS

Castelnaudary, France

*T*he town makes bricks, mostly. Castelnaudary is small and roofed with brick-red tiles. It huddles round the Canal du Midi, not far from the Black Mountain in southwestern France. Its fame comes from its *spécialité*, its dish, which is baked beans. Like the pesto of Genoa or the smoked meat and bagels of Montreal, the baked beans of Castelnaudary have acquired a mythical status and help to create the identity of the city that brought them to perfection.

These are the apotheosis of all baked beans, everywhere, and like most mythical dishes they are the subject of poetry, of purple patches of prose, of savage invective, and of intense historical research.

Cooked long and slowly in special local earthenware pots, white beans are enriched with pork and preserved goose, garlic, herbs, and not mere sausages but *famous* sausages, grilled and placed in a spiral just beneath the crisp brick-coloured crust that forms on the surface. There might be one crust, or two, or three, or more: that is, the original crust may be gently pushed down among the beans while a new one takes shape on top, to be pushed down in turn and so on.

In the nineteenth century, trains stopping at Castelnaudary station were invaded at once by the heady perfume of cassoulet, and the vendors' cries of "Alleluia! Alleluia!" The latter is the name of a long, sugared, rather plain and dry cake which can still be bought, exclusively, at the Pâtisserie Belloc in the rue 11 novembre.

The fights and the feverish research go on because two other towns, Toulouse and Carcassonne, have the effrontery to claim that *they* invented the special baked bean. In an earnest effort to achieve reconciliation, Prosper Montagné, native of Castelnaudary and compiler of the *Larousse Gastronomique*, suggested that one could think of three *equal* cassoulets—the Father (Castelnaudary), the Son (Carcassonne), and the lightest and most intellectual one, the Holy Spirit (Toulouse).

Like a great many mythic dishes, cassoulet is traditionally said to have been created entirely by accident, and during a war. In besieged, almost starving Castelnaudary, the townspeople collected all the food they could find, mixed it up in the local pottery containers, and baked it in the dying bread ovens. They sat down together and ate it and then, filled with courage, rushed from the city walls and conquered the foe. The besieging army were the English under the Black Prince; the date was 1355.

There are two main problems with the story. First, the Black Prince succeeded in invading Castelnaudary and pillaged and burned the town. Second, white beans came from America—long after 1355. Mexican Indians have cultivated and eaten white beans for at least 3,000 years. The Aztec word for them was *ayacotl*, which the Spanish reported as *haricot*. Different kinds of haricots were sent to Pope Clement VII, who in 1528 gave them to the Italian botanist and priest Pietro Valeriano, and he pronounced them excellent food.

When Catherine de Médicis went to France she took haricot beans with her. The Lauragais, the area of which Castelnaudary was capital, became her personal property. It is thought to have been Catherine who was officially responsible for the enthusiastic reception of this vegetable in the region.

A strange linguistic coincidence ties up the tale of the haricot bean and the pre-Columbian legend of the stew of the Lauragais. The people already had a stew, an ancient concoction of turnips and mutton, the name of which was *halicot* or *haricot*, probably from a word meaning "cut in pieces." There was also a venerable tradition of mixing European broad beans (favas) with chopped meat.

Today the streets of Castelnaudary still reek deliciously of cassoulet. There are at least six cassoulet canning factories. It is true that even here "light" cuisine has struck, reducing the quantities of cassoulet eaten, and eliminating a good deal of the *couenne* (pork rind) and other fats that anointed the original beans.

The official recipe for cassoulet—*couenne, andouilles,* and all—is given to every passing traveller who will accept one. It has been approved by the Grande Confrérie of the Cassoulet: thirty-seven Chevaliers, many Peers, and a horde of Dignitaries. They take an oath, in Occitan, the langue d'oc, to "defend the quality and the glory of cassoulet for life." They are robed for ceremonies in brick-red, cassoulet-crust-coloured velvet with golden, ermine-tipped scapulars, and coiffed with conical caps in the shape of the original *cassole* or cassoulet pot, the gift to the world of the village of Ussel, just north of Castelnaudary.

It is absolutely no good trying to follow the recipe, even though the citizens of Castelnaudary have translated it into English for us. Where is one to find, back home, the Lauragais goose ("none other will do"), the fresh *lingots* (*special* haricots, "the very best for cassoulet"), the extraordinary sausage? A cooling brick bread oven is essential, and it must be "heated with odorous gorse from the Black Mountain." In any case, the recipe further confirms the mythical status of the dish when it warns us that we cannot hope to succeed without what it calls the "indefinite" properties of the Castelnaudary water.

Bibliography

Elizabeth David, *French Country Cooking*. London: John Lehmann, 1951, pp. 92–94.

Elizabeth David, *French Provincial Cooking*. London: Michael Joseph, 1960, p. 450.

Francis Falcou, *Le Cassoulet de Castelnaudary*. Toulouse: Loubatières, 1986.

Prosper Montagné, *Le festin occitan*. Carcassonne, 1954.

Maguelonne Toussaint-Samat, *Histoire naturelle et morale de la nourriture*. Paris: Bordas, 1987, pp. 45–46.

IN FLAGRANTE DELICTO

The reason why the lobster blushed, according to one of the hoariest of riddles, was because "he saw the salad dressing." This answer, satisfying as it is at a certain level, deserves a closer look. For one thing, why should the lobster be the one to blush? We do not hear of the salad blushing, do we?

The lobster is red entirely because we have boiled him (alive, as a matter of fact). But we are distracted at once from this unpleasant realization by the picture of a salad dressing—that is, a salad half-undressed. Since salad, in our culture, comes equipped with ready "female" connotations, she has been seen dressing presumably by a male—one grotesquely different from herself, but soon to be paired remorselessly with her as somebody's lunch.

But even before we get to the salad, the lobster *blushes*,

and that makes him unequivocally human. Only people blush; animals never do. Animals flush—but that is something entirely different. They go red to frighten enemies and prey, and the passion they feel is anger, or lust, or triumph. (People flush for these reasons too; a Roman general celebrating a triumph would have his face painted a brilliant ritual scarlet.)

No creature on earth but a human being will relax the muscular coatings of the small arteries in its face, thereby causing its capillaries to fill with blood, all because of committing—and all unwilling!—a social impropriety. It is not that our fabulous lobster has gone red because he has done anything morally wrong. He has merely broken a rule of etiquette; his blush shows that he knows it, and wishes it had not been so.

To blush is often to disarm the hostility of others, for blushing demonstrates a desire to please, to submit to society's hegemony over us. It is therefore often deemed to be a sign of innocence, humility, or perceptiveness: only the "brazen-faced" do not blush. "No man," wrote Dr Johnson, "finds in himself any inclination to attack or oppose him who confesses his superiority by blushing in his presence."

People sensitive to the proprieties will blush even at the sight of someone else's faux pas: they imagine what they themselves would feel if caught in the other's position, and their faces "burn" in sympathy. Our salad remains unrepentantly green, however: she is nonchalant (unheated) and keeps her sang-froid. ("Blush" is from the same root as "blaze.")

A modern structuralist in the tradition of Lévi-Strauss (author of *The Raw and the Cooked*) might then reflect that the lobster has undergone the ultimate civilizing transformation in being cooked (only human beings cook their food). But the salad—female, structureless, untamed hussy that she is—remains appallingly cool and raw.

Faces blush, and less often necks and chests. "Face" is what we call the image of ourselves that we present to others: "face" can be maintained or (disastrously) lost. But the word is related to "facade," which is thought of in our culture as an often deceitful cover-up. We tend to place so high a value upon sincerity that in an important sense blushing earns our approval just because it can destroy facade. Reddening out of embarrassment is entirely involuntary, and, what is more, cannot be feigned. Blushing has often been taken to prove that the body may react directly to the mind, even beyond the individual's conscious will.

Another thing that could be troubling the lobster is the possibility that the salad might expect him to act upon his new intimacy with her. He might be reddening from apprehension, uncertainty, or unwillingness. In any of these cases he must be wondering whatever to do next. One thing he can be sure of is that he can never be again, in her eyes, the lobster he was.

Blushing is caused by intense attention to oneself, and especially to oneself in the eyes and expectations of other people. Any attempt to relieve a blusher's confusion may therefore simply make him or her turn redder still by heightening the degree of self-attention and the awareness of other people's noticing it.

The difference between a human blush and an animal flush is mainly that animals are not conscious, as we are, of the self and of social norms. Human infants never blush either: reddening with shame begins when the child is learning the myriad rules he must know and at least try to keep if he is to cut a figure in his social world.

We blush out of a passionate need to maintain our carefully constructed image of ourselves: most blushing occurs when we sense that we cannot measure up to other people's expectations of us—especially when those expectations arise from the image we have been trying to project.

We blush above all (reflexive complexity is the nature of the phenomenon) when we think that other people think that we are different from what we want them to think we are.

Bibliography

Thomas H. Burgess, *The Physiology or Mechanism of Blushing....* London: J. Churchill, 1839.

Charles Darwin, *The Expression of Emotions in Man and Animals.* London: Watts, 1948 (originally published 1872), last chapter.

Erving Goffman, *Interaction Ritual.* Garden City, New York: Doubleday, 1967.

Samuel Johnson, *The Rambler,* Number 159 (Tuesday, 24 September 1751). In W.J. Bate and Albrecht B. Strauss, eds., *The Yale Edition of the Works of Samuel Johnson,* Vol. V. New Haven and London: Yale University Press, 1969, p. 82.

Claude Lévi-Strauss, *Le cru et le cuit.* Paris: Plon, 1964. Trans. John and Doreen Weightman, *The Raw and the Cooked.* New York: Harper and Row, 1969.

TIPS OF THE SLONGUE

A Canadian radio announcer recently offered to "wake May for the news." It wasn't a *very* good spoonerism, but it had the advantage of total involuntariness. Nothing is quite as funny as catching ourselves, or others, in the act—in this case, of committing a verbal slip transposing two words, or the initial sounds of two words, and so creating an entirely correct but very different sentence.

The man whose name became synonymous with this ancient form of humorous lapse was called William Archibald Spooner. He was a member of New College, Oxford, for sixty-two years from 1862 to 1924, as undergraduate, Fellow, Tutor, Dean, and finally Warden. His contribution to scholarship was an edition of the *Histories* of Tacitus (1891).

Julian Huxley, who was for six years a Fellow under him, described Spooner as a man who "worked very hard, without any thought of self, and gave the impression of possessing that rare quality which I can only describe as saintliness." He was a tiny albino, with a disproportionately large head and very short-sighted pale blue eyes.

Some say he never uttered a spoonerism in his life; if so, he was a very unusual man indeed. Others report that he made reversals and confusions not only of speech and writing, but also of action. A.J. Toynbee recalled that he once spilled salt on the table, and responded by reaching for a bottle of wine and pouring it onto the salt. (Adding salt to spilled wine is a good way of preventing a wine stain.)

The Warden once met Stanley Casson, the future archaeologist, and asked him to dinner to meet "our new Fellow, Casson." "But Warden, I *am* Casson." "Never mind," said Spooner, "come all the same." It is certain that his extremely poor eyesight lay at the bottom of many of his most mysterious pronouncements.

Spooner became the stuff of legend, which grew and multiplied with the help of his colleagues and students. He probably never did ask a Roman Catholic for a prescription of the dope, address a crowd of farmers as noble tons of soil, compliment his hostess on her nosy little cook, or offer to sew a woman to her sheet. On one occasion, toasting Queen Victoria at a College function, he is said to have raised his glass to the queer old Dean.

Spooner was an Anglican priest, and many prize

spoonerisms are claimed to have occurred during his sermons. "Which of us," he demanded, "has not discovered in his heart a half-warmed fish?" The Prodigal Son he described as being on the busy drink of destruction. And "Yes indeed," he intoned, "the Lord is a shoving leopard."

Spoonerisms are very old, though the earliest recorded one found so far in English dates only to 1622. They are common in all languages. But the *naming* of the phenomenon—Spooner was only in his fifties when his name was adopted as a common noun and thereby immortalized—is late nineteenth century.

Even before Freud gave his name to the Slip which reveals thoughts we cannot or would rather not disclose, an Austrian professor called Rudolf Meringer set solemnly about collecting verbal errors among his colleagues at the University of Vienna.

He would stop his interlocutor in mid-sentence, write down the speaker's error, then his date of birth, name, state of fatigue, and his level of education *if lower than that of a professor.* He reported the exact linguistic context of the verbal lapse, why the speaker thought he had made it, and what he had recently read, heard, and said.

In this manner Meringer collected 4,400 slips of the tongue, including many spoonerisms. It is a corpus which is still the most valued source for linguistic research in the field, and especially appreciated because Meringer had no theories to push—he simply collected mistakes. We are also told that he was the most unpopular man of his day at the University of Vienna.

The Reverend Dr Spooner, on the other hand, was loved by everyone—but then he is remembered for making errors, not for collecting them. We cannot help revering a man who rode a well-boiled icicle, a man whom we can even imagine saying: "You have hissed all my mystery lectures. I saw you fight a liar in the quad. In fact, you have tasted a whole worm. Please pack up your rags and your bugs, and depart by the town drain."

Bibliography

Victoria Fromkin, "The Non-Anomalous Nature of Anomalous Utterance," *Language* 47 (1971) 27–52.

Victoria Fromkin, ed., *Speech Errors as Linguistic Evidence.* The Hague: Mouton, 1973.

Victoria Fromkin, ed., *Errors in Linguistic Performance: Slips of the Tongue, Ear, Pen and Hand.* New York: Academic Press, 1980.

William Hayter, *Spooner: A Biography.* London: W.H. Allen, 1977.

Julian Huxley, *On Living in a Revolution.* London: Chatto and Windus, 1944.

Rudolf Meringer and K. Mayer, *Versprechen und Verlesen: Eine Psychologisch-linguistische Studie.* Stuttgart: Göschensche Verlag, 1895.

Rudolf Meringer, *Aus dem Leben der Sprache: Versprechen, Kindersprache, Nachahmungstrieb.* Berlin: Behr's Verlag, 1908.

R.H. Robbins, "The Warden's Wordplay: Towards a Redefinition of the Spoonerism," *Dalhousie Review* 46 (1966) 457–65.

GREETINGS

*K*issing has been unacceptable as an everyday ritual salutation in Anglo-Saxon culture ever since the 1830s. To greet one's friends by kissing them in public is a mark of "Continental" extravagance—along with shoulder-shrugging, constant hand-shaking, and gesticulation in general.

But perhaps this is now changing. More and more people seem to be greeting each other by kissing. It is all very conscious still—one often cannot know whether to kiss or not to kiss, or how to do it correctly. A little anxious dance follows the hurried "Hi's"—which side first? Is it to be two kisses or only one? Or even three?

Whether the tendency will spread or last is impossible to foretell. But it surely arises from the realization that our mores are really very cold and "unphysical" compared with those of many other human cultures. Contempt for the emotionalism and theatricality conventionally shown by Latin people, for instance, is giving way among us to admiration for their apparently comforting ritual demonstrations of warmth.

Greetings are classed by social anthropologists as "access rituals." They even count, because many animals perform them assiduously, as access "displays." When two people greet each other they are ceremoniously granting, and publicly demonstrating, increased access to each other's person, and to attention, time, and consideration. Simultaneously, they may be celebrating differences in social hierarchy.

The history of greeting, in many if not most cultures, shows a continuous decline in formality. The most important people could, at certain times and places, command prostration (often three times) as a greeting, together with kissing the dust and kissing of their feet.

In medieval Europe, prostrations were replaced by kneeling. A man knelt on two knees to God, on one to his superiors; women knelt on both knees to people as well as God. Such kneeling was called, for both men and women, a "curtsy," from the word *courtesy*, originally meaning behaviour refined enough to be practised by courtiers. "Bowing" meant bending the knees.

With the arrival of the Victorian age, the English—who had once been the talk of Europe because English men commonly kissed all women on the mouth as a greeting— ceased kissing in public altogether. The curtsy (now a knee-bend confined to women) and the bow (men were keeping their knees rigid and lowering the torso instead) were reserved only for formal occasions. Everyone began shaking hands as an everyday greeting.

Hand-shaking ("the American shake-hand," the French contemptuously called it) had since classical times meant honour, solemn friendship, and the forming of a contract. Using the right hand for it showed peace and benevolence: you had no intention of drawing your sword. This ancient formality declined into much smaller change. Eventually the French themselves adopted it. They now shake hands constantly, whenever kissing on both cheeks is deemed either too elaborate or too intimate: every time somebody is introduced to a group, or leaves it, he or she must shake hands all round.

Lifting the right hand to the head as a salute derived in part from the traditional male reverential greetings of tugging forelocks and raising hats. The latter was called "uncovering"; the head remained hatless until one was told by one's superior to cover it again. It used to be the custom for upper-class boys to bow and take off their hats, and for girls to curtsy, every time they saw their parents. (In the East it is respectful to "uncover" too, except that you bare your feet instead of your head.)

Showing that the right hand was holding no weapon was probably one origin of our habit of waving; another is said to have been the polite raising of the right arm to make room when passing others in narrow lanes. Pushing back visors and hoods to facilitate recognition of one's face may have led to hat-tipping as well as waving and saluting, and the ancient praying gesture, fist to forehead, looks like another forerunner of the salute.

Spoken greetings were always far more complex than the modern "Hello" and "Hi." ("Hello" derives from calling animals; "Hi" may be short for "Hiyah," or "How are you?") But an enquiry as to whether someone is well need hardly mean what it says: "How do you do?" is never answered, except by another "How do you do?", which requires no response. Such phrases are "access rituals" merely.

But woe betide anyone who does not greet, or who is judged not to greet with sufficient warmth. In *Conversational Routine* (1981), Charles Ferguson, Professor of Linguistics at Stanford, describes an "informal experiment" he once conducted. When he arrived at work one day he greeted his secretary's "Good morning" with a silent smile, then strove to remain as nearly normal as possible after that lapse on first meeting. Next day he did the same. Tension mounted as his inadequate greetings continued; he received "strange looks" from his colleagues.

Very soon his nerves failed, and he dropped the experiment: he was "afraid of the explosion," and of the possible lasting consequences of his not fully participating in this small, endlessly repeated ritual of sociability, which people think little about, but which they nevertheless relentlessly exact.

Bibliography

Florian Coulmas, ed., *Conversational Routine: Explorations in Standardized Communication Situations and Prepatterned Speech.* The Hague: Mouton, 1981.

Erving Goffman, *Relations in Public: Microstudies of the Public Order.* New York: Basic Books, 1971.

Joan Wildeblood, *The Polite World: A Guide to the Deportment of the English in Former Times.* Revised ed. London: Davis-Poynter, 1973.

BEARDS

*T*he human male has always revered his chin. In the
hairy races, such as the Caucasian, male chins produce beards. This means that they may be shaven, unshaved,
or the hair upon them decoratively and variously clipped.
The expressive and mythic possibilities are enormous: chins
have been amorously sighed over because still smooth,
stroked to produce thought, and beards either plucked as the
ultimate disgrace or sworn upon in taking oaths.

Beards arrive with puberty, so they inevitably represent
male potency, and male sexuality in general. But old men,
who often lose the hair on the tops of their heads, keep it
on their chins. This has been a source of great satisfaction;
and men as they age often choose to wear longer and
bushier beards than young men do.

A man may grow a beard to mark a turning point in his

life, or to show that he is waiting for a change ("I shall not shave until..."). He might also wear one as a symbolic shield, to hide behind. An antishaving tract (1860) called the beard "a divinely provided chest-protector"—but found it necessary to add, "Were it in any other position, its benefit and purpose might be doubted."

Two favourite metaphors for beards are of water and "flowing" (classical river gods were richly bearded males), and of flowers and "flourishing." Charlemagne was famous for having "*la barbe fleurie*," and the word for producing a beard in ancient Greek means "flowering." Beards in another mode may be repellent (the Emperor Julian's was called "shaggy and populous" by the satirists of Antioch); or threatening, and compared with knives, axes, or spades.

Chins have been used as badges of status. Ancient Egyptians were chic if they shaved all over, so that hairiness was lower-class. (Important Egyptians, however, tied metal beards to their chins on ceremonial occasions: even women wore these if they were *very* high up.) When the upper class was bearded, as among the frizzed and anointed Assyrians, poorer people were often forced to shave. Several times in history, men had either to pay a tax on their beards or to shave them off, the pleasures of beardedness being restricted to those who could afford them.

Beards were one thing women could not have—which was of course part of the charm for their possessors. Bearded ladies were freaks of the circus. But women had a saint they could implore if they wished to avoid unwanted masculine attentions. She was St Wilgefortis, a determined Portuguese woman who prayed to be delivered from men, and was delighted when she found she had sprouted a full beard. Englishwomen called her St Uncumber, and Frenchwomen prayed for her help as Ste Débarras.

A large beard can look heavily significant: of years, of broad and intricate knowledge, and of vigorous commitment to something beyond the trivial concerns of the rest of us. Revolutionary and prophetic beards have been worn in recent times by radicals from John Lennon to the Ayatollah Khomeini, while Marxist iconography included an image of Lenin, Marx, and Engels—the Three Founders—overlapping, beard upon beard.

But even men not aspiring to the prophetic have tended to consider their beards both sacred and precious. The Anglo-Saxon fine for spoiling a beard was calculated at twenty silver pieces, compared with twelve for breaking a thigh. Beards have been threaded with gold, jewelled, beribboned and curled; and men have gone to bed with their beards in bags and wooden presses to protect the styling. We all remember the oath of the little pig confronting the wolf's entreaties: "No, no, by the hair on my chinny-chin-chin!"

Young people often complain that the old ramble on and on. The French exclaim *"Quelle barbe!"* ("What a beard!") when they are bored; southern Europeans popularly express this in graphic silence, by pinching their chins, or sketching onto them a beard with their hands.

Not very long ago, beards were rarely seen in our society, and wearing one was shockingly non-conformist behaviour. But men now feel as free to choose beardedness as they do the clean-shaven state. Those who wish to look tough, and dangerous because uncategorizable within social conventions, have very little opportunity to make their point, as it were, with their chins.

One can still cut a disturbing figure, however, by being *neither* clean-shaven *nor* bearded. People are forced to wonder about motivations for an unmistakable stubble: is this man growing a beard for a reason (but what could it be?), or is he too busy, too miserable, too aggressive, or too socially out of tune to shave? Whatever the case, he is, at least temporarily, not one of us; his transitory, prickly, ambiguous chin is both intriguing and uncomfortable to see.

Bibliography

William E. Addison, "Beardedness as a Factor in Perceived Masculinity," *Perceptual and Motor Skills* 68 (1989) 921–22.

Edward Clodd, "Beards," in James Hastings, ed., *Encyclopaedia of Religion and Ethics.* New York: Charles Scribner, 1913, Vol. 2, pp. 441–43.

Wendy Cooper, *Hair.* New York: Stein and Day, 1971.

The Emperor Julian, *Misopogon* (*"The Beard-Hater"*) 338c–339b. Written in AD. 361–362. *The Works of the Emperor Julian.* Trans. Wilmer Cave Wright. London: Heinemann, 1913, pp. 420–511.

Reginald Reynolds, *Beards.* Garden City, New York: Doubleday, 1949.

"Theologos," *Shaving a breach of the Sabbath and a hindrance to the spread of the Gospel.* 1860. (Quoted in Clodd, above.)

Douglas R. Wood, "Self-Perceived Masculinity between Bearded and Nonbearded Males," *Perceptual and Motor Skills* 62 (1986) 769–70.

AVOCADOS

*H*igh in the cloud forests of northern South America, the fruit grows to the size of a large olive; it is beloved of two-toed sloths and named by botanists *nubigena*, "the cloud-born." In the region of Mount Popacatapetl, Mexican Indians worked long and hard upon another race of the same tree and perfected a somewhat larger, thin-skinned, purple version, with a scent like anise. These two, hybridized in pre-Columbian times, eventually created the big green avocado usually for sale in northern cities today.

The purple parent is the most ancient cultivated one; it was being grown by the peoples of Central America before 7000 BC. Gradually the fruit improved through selection, but avocado trees grow so slowly and their seeds produce so erratically that a sudden great leap forward in the fruit's size, which occurred around 900 BC, is considered to be proof of a significant increase in social organization among the people who produced them.

The results are still popular in Mexico today, and their taste is greatly preferred among gourmets who have tried all the varieties. But "Mexican" avocados are not exported north, both because they are small and because their thin skins make them difficult to transport without bruising. The ones we get are crossed with the "Guatemalan" type, direct descendants of the wild and thick-skinned *nubigena.*

There is one more domesticated type of avocado—the so-called "West Indian," which also originated in Mexico. It is a tropical version (the other two are subtropical), and the trees now flourish in the Caribbean, in Florida, in Africa, and in other hot parts of the world. The one growing in our garden in Zambia was nearly sixty feet tall. This fruit's skin is purple, and you can tell the fruit is ripe because its pip loosens: you shake it, and take it if you hear the pip bumping around inside.

Tropical avocados are only three to ten per cent fat, as opposed to anything up to thirty per cent in the types preferring cooler conditions. There is more oil in avocados than in any other fruit except olives. The oil is highly digestible, and chemically very like olive oil; its main use so far is in cosmetic creams. Avocados, like grapefruit, have become for us a popular pre-dinner appetizer; but in Brazil they are preferred sugared and eaten for dessert.

The fruit is an anomaly in many ways. Maturation, for instance, does not change its skin colour, and the fruit does not soften until it has left the tree. Readiness for harvesting is therefore determined by trial and error, or by chemical tests for oil content. A mature avocado can be "stored" for weeks, and sometimes up to seven months, simply by being left on the tree. Picking the fruit cuts off the hormone (produced in the leaves) that prevents it from ripening.

Three or four days afterwards the avocado will be ready to eat, a state recognizable when it is slightly soft at the stem end; but this happens only if it has (imperceptibly) matured on the tree. Mild refrigeration keeps the fruit another month or so after harvesting. But the avocado, unlike any other fruit, needs oxygen in order to ripen without spoiling; it must not be wrapped up while it is metabolizing. Another rule is that fruit usually sweetens as it matures; but the ripening process in the avocado actually *reduces* sugar content, to as little as one per cent.

Animals, even carnivores, love avocados. Père Labat describes in his Caribbean journal (1693–1705) how wild pigs from miles around would congregate under the avocado trees when a windstorm had shaken the fruit to the ground. "These animals," he wrote, "become in consequence marvellously plump, and their flesh contracts an excellent savour."

Dipping chips and bits of vegetable into a centrally placed bowl of sauce is a distinctively North American table trait. The practice expresses informality, individuality, and egalitarianism, of course—but it may also derive historically from the American Indian habit of adding enriching sauces to the corn staple of the region: corn needs supplements in order to be adequately nutritious. One of the best sauce-making fruits on earth was ready to hand in Central America: the buttery, mashable, protein- and vitamin-rich avocado. Modern North Americans discovered it relatively recently; when they did, their dipping habit was already ingrained.

Europe received its first large supplies from Israel in the 1970s. Israelis have heartily adopted and promoted them, developing special harvesting machinery, experimenting with recipes, and introducing the idea of weaning babies on avocado flesh.

The name of the fruit in Spanish is *aguacate*, earlier *ahuacate*, fruit of *ahuacacuahatl*, the Aztec "testicle tree": pear-shaped fruit hang from the tree in pairs. *Avocado* may also have been influenced by the Spanish word for a delicacy, *bocado*. When Jamaicans received the avocado, nearly 300 years before North Americans began seriously growing it, they turned *ahuacate* into *alligator* because the word had an easier and more familiar sound.

North Americans popularly called them *alligator pears* until marketers decided the connotations were a turn-off, and pushed the term *avocado*. Indian claims for aphrodisiac powers in the fruit were hotly denied when it was first being introduced widely in North America at the beginning of this century; the reputation is no longer thought by the industry to be a liability.

Bibliography

Jean-Baptiste Labat, *Voyage aux îles de l'Amérique (1693–1705)*. Paris: Séghers, 1979, (first published 1722) pp. 92–93.

Harold McGee, *On Food and Cooking*. New York: Charles Scribner's Sons, 1984, pp. 202–203.

Waverley Root, *Food*. New York: Simon and Schuster, 1980, pp. 17–18.

C. Earle Smith Jr., "Archaeological Evidence for Selection in Avocado," *Economic Botany* 20 (1966) 169–75.

C. Earle Smith Jr., "Additional Notes on Pre-Conquest Avocados in Mexico," *Economic Botany* 23 (1969) 135–40.

Wessel Smitter, "The Mysterious Avocado," *Saturday Evening Post*, February 26, 1949, pp. 30ff.

Louis O. Williams, "The Avocados: A Synopsis of the Genus *Persea*, subg. *Persea*," *Economic Botany* 31 (1977) 315–20.

TIPPING

*H*airdressers snip round our ears and run fingers over our scalps, car valets park our Porsches, postmen carry mail to our own front doors, tour guides lead us over mountain passes and through spicy bazaars, telling us what to look at and helping us find rest rooms on the way. We do not usually know any of these people personally, yet we are forced, at least temporarily or from time to time, to depend on them and to trust them utterly. At the end of the journey or the session or the year's services, we give a tip.

Many of us do this with very bad grace, feeling uncertain what to give and how, and even suspecting that we are being obscurely had. We wish it did not have to be done, persuaded as we are nowadays that self-sufficiency is the ultimate goal, and that we should limit and control everything that comes in contact with our persons. But in spite of every modern discouragement, the tipping convention survives.

Doctors were once regarded as part of this legion of lowly yet annoyingly powerful people who deal with us at our most vulnerable, and can therefore command a special reward. So were lawyers, teachers, and others. But in the course of the nineteenth century these groups banded together and called themselves professionals, and they are now able to prove to us just how dangerous and overbearing they are by demanding—and exacting—fees large enough to be felt.

Long gone is the day when a surgeon's job was described by gentlemen as "a crude affair of the knife," or when lawyers wore purses between their shoulder blades, to catch the largesse dropped into them by lordly clients. (The puckering at the back of a lawyer's robe is a vestige of this money bag.) Professionals have seen to it that the public should never again condescend when paying up, and should seldom utter a complaint; professionals no longer receive tips.

That the word "tip" is an acronym for "To Insure Promptness" is a myth. "Tip" means "give"; a "gratuity" is gratuitously given. A "service charge" is therefore not a tip but merely an addition to the bill; it is a cunning subversion of tipping, whereby employees are assured of their extra sum (but have their wages lowered accordingly), and are forced to use their personal contact with the customer to make him or her spend more: ten per cent of a hundred and thirty dollars is more than ten per cent of eighty.

Tips are given where the service is *personal,* and in this they resemble professional fees. They show appreciation for trustworthiness and extra attention, both of them demonstrated just where infinite trouble could arise if the ministrant turned unwilling.

Someone who cuts your nails without bloodshed—who actually makes your fingers look better, not worse—has given you something extra, something to be relieved about. Enormous skill is not the point; nor is unique gift-edness. Tips are supposed to be for something salaries cannot reward; they symbolize recognition for a finally unenforceable personal effort.

Tip-receivers judge, classify, and often manage to manipulate the people from whom, as waiters still say, they "take orders." They firmly believe, for instance, that men are likely to tip more than women, and will often, therefore, take more notice of men. If a man has a woman with him, all the better: he is likely to want to show off to her by tipping generously.

Waiters suppose women dining alone to be unimpressed by service: they are used themselves to serving without being paid for it, and probably have less money anyway. Older people are thought of as better tippers, less likely to "stiff" (not pay a tip), than younger ones: they are usually richer, more experienced, more old-fashioned, and therefore more amenable to social pressure.

People with children are the worst. They have the least money to begin with, and children might mean more work—for a lower tip. People on holiday package tours are bad too: economy has led them to take the tour in the first place, and they go on to think that their fee has paid in advance for everything—porters, guides, and waiters included.

In spite of the personal relationship symbolized by a tip, people who receive tips are often regarded, on the job, as non-persons. Taxi-drivers' fares commonly discuss their personal lives and finances, kiss, curse, and fight in the back of a cab as though the driver's seat were empty. Waiters are supposed not to sit, eat, drink, or talk to each other within sight of customers: ideally they are gliding, murmuring automata, swift but scarcely human.

The bestowal of tips gives modern people one of the rare opportunities left them to behave as the nobility once did, for the gentry were taught to pretend that any members of the lower orders who were in their presence, and upon whom they depended, were not really there.

Bibliography

O.E. Bigus, "The Milkman and His Customer," *Urban Life and Culture* 1 (1972) 131–66.

F. Davis, "The Cabdriver and His Fare," *American Journal of Sociology* 65 (1959) 158–65.

R.L. Karen, "Some Factors Affecting Tipping Behaviour," *Sociology and Social Research* 47 (1962) 68–74.

Gerald Mars and Michael Nicod, *The World of Waiters*. London: Allen and Unwin, 1984.

Philip Nailon, "Tipping: A Behavioural Review," *Hotel and Catering Institute Management Association Review* 2 (1978) 231–43.

William Joseph Reader, *Professional Men: The Rise of the Professional Classes in Nineteenth-Century England*. London: Weidenfeld and Nicolson, 1966.

VACATIONS

North Americans work extremely hard, for long hours, and with remarkably short holidays. If we compare our employment patterns with the workday of a hunter-gatherer in the Peruvian forests (three to four hours), the average work week in pre-revolutionary France (four days), or the annual number of work-free days in fourth-century Rome (a hundred and seventy-five), we seem a very hard-driven lot.

In modern France, no employer is allowed to offer workers less than five weeks' vacation per year, and most people take more than that. Ten working days is Canada's minimum allotment, a miserly one by any standard. (Saskatchewan is the exception, with fifteen working days off.) And yet we rarely hear people complain.

One reason is that in North America one can earn good

money for working, and people have often felt they would rather have more money than more free time. Another is that we tend to compare our lot with what we had in our own recent past. If we look back at the nineteenth century, we are certainly better off now. Then, the average worker put in seventy hours per week; a shopkeeper normally worked eighty-four. At one point in England there were exactly two days' holiday per year, apart from Sundays.

Yet the idea of taking holidays *en bloc*—first one week, then two—took well over a century to be accepted, after it was first mooted in the 1790s. And employers had virtually to force workers to accept the deal.

Until the end of the eighteenth century, "holidays" were holy days, days of local celebration and festivity. On top of these, there were political events for which one could down tools, and also less strictness about absenteeism. People worked seasonally—very hard indeed when it was necessary, and not at all when it was not. Modern factory management can put up with none of that. Regularity and predictability are the name of the game, and everything has been done to phase out seasons. The machines that free us from work keep us very busy indeed.

Nineteenth-century factory owners saw that it suited them better to tell their workers exactly when they could stay at home—which limited block of time they could have—than never to know when they would not show up for work. But what employers could not stomach was the idea of paying people while they were not working. People sold their labour as though it was merchandise, and the workers themselves appear to have accepted this view of what they had to offer. Block holidays were often imposed on employees, who had also to forgo their wages while they "rested." Meanwhile, most festivals—the traditional days off—had been abolished.

The new concept—block holidays with pay—is one of the hallmarks of modernity, and it has no precedent in history. It is being increasingly recognized by historians that Nazism, Fascism, and Communism were in many respects not aberrations but experiments in modernity, roads (fortunately) not taken. It was the Nazis and Fascists, in Germany and Italy in the 1920s, who were first fully to embrace the notion that workers should be paid during their block holidays. The idea was born in late-nineteenth-century Britain, but the British Holidays With Pay Act dates only from 1938.

Mussolini's regime invented what was called *dopolavoro*, "after-work": employees were to use the new transport facilities and get away on organized trips. Spontaneity would be contained, instruction provided, and entertainment laid on. Bodies were to be exercised, "recreated." Modern work is mostly bad for bodies, so efficiency could be expected to improve.

The workers themselves often did not *want* to go away, or be organized. They mostly preferred to stay at home, and to rest when they wanted to. They would have chosen, in most instances, shorter hours over a couple of weeks off.

Even today, many workers would much rather take odd days off than have to keep their noses to the grindstone until the one annual vacation period rolls round.

Yet the iron link between work and holidays remains, enshrined as it is in the way we speak about them. When *on leave* we leave off working, but only when we are given leave to do so—and we often leave town then as well. Holy days used to be filled with activity and heavy with significance; they have been replaced by *vacations*, literally "empty" times—emptied, that is, of work. *Retiring* means ceasing to go to work. And *recreation* gets you ready for more work.

Those who can get away, do: work is hard, boring, and repetitive, and we feel we must escape. It also suits the powers that be to give us a stretch of time in which to spend the money we devote most of our lives to earning. Vacations and "leisure" are vast money-making industries in themselves. And we have become so pleased with our holidays, yearning for them all year long as we do, that we would be outraged if anyone tried to take them away from us. We think of them now as the time we have to enjoy ourselves, when we are really and truly alive—as compared with the rest of our existence, and by far the greater part of it, that we spend at work.

Bibliography

John A.R. Pimlott, *The Englishman's Holiday: A Social History*. London: Faber and Faber, 1947.

Jean Viard, *Penser les vacances*. Paris: Actes Sud, 1984.

ENGLISH SPELLING; OR WOULD YOU LIKE TO BE PHTHEIGHCHOUND FOR A GHOTI?

*W*e can all take comfort in the realization that *nobody* thinks English spelling is easy. For four and a half centuries, those who have resented its complexities have fought for simplification and reform. They have wanted to take it upon themselves to regularize patterns, cut out letters, remove exceptions, or replace the alphabet altogether. George Bernard Shaw could not understand why we should wish to live with a language in which *fish* might as well be spelled *ghoti* (f as in cou*gh*, i as in w*o*men, and sh as in na*ti*on). *Taken* comes out as *phtheighchound* (*phth*isic, w*eigh*, s*ch*ool, glam*ou*r, and han*dso*me).

Yet only two men have ever had any lasting effect on English spelling rules: Samuel Johnson (who got to choose among alternatives when writing his dictionary), and Noah Webster (another lexicographer, who made Americans change -*our* to -*or*, and gave them *liter*, *traveling*, and *catalog*). English (and American) spelling is now known to rank with Gaelic in complexity—at the other end of the scale from Finnish and Serbo-Croatian, which have the most regular spelling of all. Why then have we not rationalized our spelling system? What are we waiting for?

English spelling *is* a system, and even English spelling is mostly regular: eighty-four per cent of words are straightforward, thirteen per cent decently rule-abiding, and only three per cent so weird that we have no choice but to memorize them. But among those three per cent are 400 of the commonest words in the language: *gone*, *done*, *of*, and so on. These weigh heavily against the relative simplicity of the rest. But they are the last words anyone wants to change. The moment a spelling reformer writes *ov*, we oppose him: English abhors words ending in *v*.

The assumption most people make is that *sound* is what spelling expresses. It mostly does so, of course—but the way words are written also gives clues to their *meaning*. The letters *sig* in *sign*, *signal*, *design*, and *designate* are pronounced differently in each word, but they show the common meaning that relates them.

The English system is extraordinarily sensitive to such meaningful sets of letters; where the pronunciation changes, it often keeps the semantic unit intact. We tend over time even to adjust the spelling of words to provide these clues more clearly: *leapt,* for instance, is gradually becoming *leaped* although the last letter is pronounced *t.* The pronunciation of words may change or revert because of the spelling; examples are *housewife, Rome,* and *certain* (which had come to sound like "hussif," "Room," and "sartin"). We even keep odd spellings because they express emotion by visual means alone: look at *ghastly, ghost,* and *ghoul.*

What this means is that written English is superb for *reading silently.* Reading silently is a relatively modern skill; ancient Greeks and Romans, for instance, thought of reading as something done out loud. Today, people usually read more swiftly than they could speak, and without sounding the words even to themselves. Writing performs a new and different function: it has to create patterns *for the eyes.* For example, if in the interests of phonetics we wrote *runz* but *hits,* the eyes would not pick up nearly so easily the structural clue which the system presents as the letter *s.*

It is in fact impossible to spell purely phonetically: writing is nothing like sound, and therefore could not "imitate" it. And pronunciation differs between dialects, and changes over time. If phonetics were made to govern all spelling, which dialect would be represented and so obscure the rest? Consider for example the loss in comprehensibility if "cone" and "conic" were spelled (as one "new system" suggests) *kon* and *kanik;* or if upper-class English usage imposed "hice" for "house."

The use of English, even by foreigners, does not seem to have been halted by difficulties in reading and writing it. This is because its spelling system, no less than its grammar and vocabulary, is sensitive, systematic, economical, and able both to resist and to accommodate change. (Usage does change, but gradually, and with the help and consent of everybody; one of the unpleasant aspects of "spelling reform" is the megalomania of the reformers.)

English does have anomalies that are impossible to excuse: one linguistic expert complains, for example, about *repair*, *forty*, and *questionnaire*. Yet we should realize that attempts to "perfect" the system overall could impair the strengths which we are just beginning to appreciate that it possesses.

True, it remains unlikely that most of us could spell the following sentence correctly on the first attempt, without a computerized word-check, and without reading it over first: "We should accommodate the possibility of unparalleled embarrassment occurring in an eccentric physicist who endeavours, though harassed by diarrhoea, to gauge the symmetry of a horse caught gambolling in ecstasy within the precincts of a cemetery wall."

Bibliography

David Crystal, *The Cambridge Encyclopedia of Language*. Cambridge University Press, 1987, pp. 213–17.

Donald W. Cummings, *American English Spelling*. Baltimore: Johns Hopkins University Press, 1988.

Fred Walter Householder, "On the Primacy of Writing," in his *Linguistic Speculations*. Cambridge University Press, 1971.

Josef Vachek, *Written Language: General Problems and Problems of English*. The Hague: Mouton, 1973.

R.L. Venezky, "From Webster to Rice to Roosevelt," in Uta Frith, ed., *Cognitive Processes in Spelling*. London and New York: Academic Press, 1980.

UMBRELLAS

*W*hen the gentleman unfurled a large circle of green silk held taut on spokes and proceeded to walk down the street holding it up, by means of a rod, over his head, people thought he had gone completely insane. Almost nobody had seen such an object before, and flaunting it seemed eccentric and pretentious behaviour; the man was followed by crowds of jeering urchins every time he ventured out.

Jonas Hanway had first seen umbrellas in Portugal in the 1750s, and recognized their possibilities for rainy England. Women had been known to walk under umbrellas, usually carried by their servants, in England before; but Hanway was probably the first man to do so regularly. Daniel Defoe's Robinson Crusoe had carried, exotically enough, an umbrella for shade, "a great clumsy ugly goat-skin" one that the hero made after a model he had seen in "the Brazils"—the Portuguese connection again. The book had appeared in 1719, when Hanway was a child. With obstinate courage he carried his "curiously jointed" umbrella, the size of a small tent, in the streets of London for thirty years, and by the end of his life he had started a British institution.

For slowly the advantages of the new device began to win it converts, and within a few decades umbrella-carrying, even by men, was common enough to cause strikes by cab-drivers, who thought that their livelihoods might be threatened if people habitually carried portable roofs about with them.

There are two, often independent, histories for the umbrella: that of the sunshade or parasol, and that of the protector against rain or *parapluie*. Umbrellas appear to have been invented as parasols at least 3,000 years ago. They were well known in ancient Egypt, and they have been used ceremonially in north Africa from that time to this. The umbrella in Africa is often twirled and bounced up and down to create a breeze: an early English definition of one was "a sort of fan." The Chinese had perfected a collapsible model by the eleventh century BC, and the Portuguese who inspired Hanway had found umbrellas to be an ancient institution in India.

One of the parasol's great advantages (apart from its practical use) was that it took up lots of space. It isolated the personage it covered, and with fringes, glitter, and bright colours could render a body highly conspicuous in a crowd. Ordinary folk were often forbidden therefore to carry umbrellas and so detract from the great man's state, and rules would specify what colour your rank entitled you to shelter under.

Rain rather than sun bothered the people of northern Europe, but they were slow to adopt the *parapluie*. In the late Renaissance, Italian and Spanish grandees took quite naturally to the perfumed leather ones that became fashionable. It was the Italian word *ombrello*, "little shadow," that became the English *umbrella*.

But in the less exquisite north, people thought it effete for a man openly to defend himself against rain: a great-coat and broad-brimmed hat or hood should suffice. It was all right for women to protect their hats and voluminous skirts with *parapluies*, and men might occasionally use the umbrellas kept by cafés for escorting customers to their carriages. (These were the forerunners of covered walkways into smart restaurants.)

Umbrellas for men caught on only when dandyism became fashionable, and when umbrellas could be made to furl so narrowly that they resembled walking-sticks or vestigial swords. We all know the uses of umbrellas as weapons; and some of us remember what must have been the ultimate umbrella-weapon, when, in 1978, the ingenious Bulgarian secret service were believed to be using smartly furled umbrellas for poking tiny poisoned pellets into their victims as they passed them on the street.

From about 1800, the story of the *parapluie* began almost totally to diverge from that of the frilly female parasol.

Upper-class women needed such parasols as a demonstration of their delicateness of constitution, of their removal from the state of needing to work, of their horror of sun-tanned skin. A whole language evolved in the management of parasols: they could be tilted, twirled, hidden behind, or snapped decisively shut.

Parapluies were merely for practical use. In order to cut an elegant figure with one, its bearer needed to be carrying little else; and it could still be a downright disadvantage to smart dressing, suggesting as it did respectability, caution, and readiness for rain and disappointment—perhaps even the lack of one's own carriage.

Parasols died in the 1920s, as the rush to the sea and the suntan began: nobody wanted to look pale and protected any more, and frills and shyness began to seem an intolerable waste of time and effort. (Parasols might well make a return, however, now that baring one's body to the sun's rays has ceased to seem a good idea.) The spread of the private automobile depressed the demand for *parapluies*, though these are with us still.

Nowadays, most of us hardly think it is worth buying a good umbrella because we are so likely to lose it. So we put up with the kind that spring open—and sometimes off—with the touch of a button, a poor compensation for rods that are far too short. We suffer tips that fall off, nylon that rips, and ribs that snap; we seldom think enough of our umbrellas to slide them back into their sheaths when not in use. Few objects have shrunk so totally from former ceremonial distinction: it is difficult for us to believe that the king of Burma could once have gloried in the title "Lord of the Twenty-Four Umbrellas."

Bibliography

Anon., "The Poisonous Umbrella," *Time*, October 16, 1978, pp. 47–48.

T.S. Crawford, *A History of the Umbrella*. Newton Abbot: David and Charles, 1970.

Daniel Defoe, *The Life and Strange Surprising Adventures of Robinson Crusoe*. Originally published 1719. Ed. W.P. Trent. New York: Ginn, 1916. See pp. 149, 151, 165.

Carol Kennedy, "High Casualty Rate Among the Exiles," *Maclean's*, October 16, 1978, pp. 32–33.

M.C. Miller, "The Parasol: An Oriental Status-Symbol in Late Archaic and Classical Athens," *Journal of Hellenic Studies* 112 (1992) 91–105.

James Stephen Taylor, *Jonas Hanway, Founder of the Marine Society*. London and Berkeley: Scolar Press, 1985, pp. 43–44.

Fay Willey and Anthony Collings, "Death by Umbrella?" *Newsweek*, September 25, 1978, p. 66.

Shway Yoe, *The Burman: His Life and Notions*. London: Macmillan, 1882, pp. 409–10.

PARADES:
TAKING OVER THE STREET

*I*n modern cities, vehicular traffic governs everything; the only reasons for which a busy main road can be closed down are disasters, road repairs—or parades. One of the rewards of holding a parade is the elation participants feel as they take over the street; a route through a pedestrian mall would sadly diminish the grandeur. The additional snarling of traffic by the fleets of buses and cars that brought people to the parade, and the resulting frustration of drivers anywhere nearby, are merely marks of the extent to which the manifestation is making itself felt.

A parade is an extraordinary spectacle whose whole purpose is to display itself. A route is chosen, with a beginning, a significant goal, and ritual landmarks to be passed en route. Between ranks of witnesses—and nowadays before the millions watching television—the parade moves forward, with bands and uniformed marchers, floats, clowns, people dressed as animals, horsemen and horse-drawn wagons, drum majorettes, and a king or a princess (North American parades love kings and princesses) or some other ruler such as Santa Claus bringing up the rear—almost; for behind this personage will come the street-cleaners, dressed up in their usual colourful costumes, doing their best to clear up the mess and ready the road for the traffic which is impatiently waiting to recover its domain.

A parade lets a little chaos into our strictly regulated lives; it is one of the few Dionysiac outlets still sanctioned by society as a whole. This is usually controlled, often highly patriotic chaos, but it does let in the wild. For a pre-determined time, on a chosen date, and along a set route, the city suddenly becomes filled with music, flowers, beasts, and fantasy.

Clowns caper about or rush up to spectators; they are descendants of the ancient satyr figures, and the medieval "whifflers" who dressed as wild men brandishing sticks. Their job is to link the procession and the bystanders by making personal contact with the latter, and to keep the crowd not only entertained but off the parade route. They have always tended to bestow gifts; our clowns still dole out buttons, balloons, and candy to children.

Processional extravaganzas used to include famous precious objects carried along for all to see, and plenty of free wine. Giants have always been popular, especially if they can move about; an element of fright and wonder is essential to a good parade. Flowers covering the street are vegetation reclaiming the pavement; they also honour the parade that treads over them. Clothing may be flung down in the parade's path, or (for a short procession) a red carpet rolled out; a coloured line drawn on the road can mark out the parade's course.

Parades reify the ideals and the pride of a city; they also try to embody its past and its plans for the future. The floats which roll by are one of the oldest components of the parade. They are minitheatres (Dionysiac again) representing events or places, or city myths and institutions like the Fire Department or Our Hardy Pioneers. Modern North American parade floats tend to be singularly moralistic in tone, glorifying Road Safety or dedicated to "Beating the Butt."

The army and military bands are nearly always included in modern secular parades. The word *parade* itself is from a Spanish military term meaning "a time and place where the army stops" (*parada*): during the rest period it wears its regalia and performs its drill for the townsfolk.

Exotic costumes, animals, floats representing distant places, or figures arriving "from afar"—like Santa Claus—symbolically inject what is "outside" into the city. Ritual reversals are another Dionysiac device. An extraordinary modern example of this is the corps of drum majorettes: women dressed as men, aggressively booted and helmeted, marching yet thereby displaying their legs, and tossing their batons in the air—*women*, actually *playing* with the symbols of power and attack.

Parades are not always cheerful celebrations: religious processions can be very solemn, and funerals incorporate a form of parade. Political demonstrations almost invariably involve parading, but care is taken by participants to distinguish these from anything resembling pageantry. In tune with the puritanical modern attitude that anything involving costume or fantasy cannot be *serious*, people in political processions usually pretend to be eschewing ritual.

This they do ritually, by dressing in the toughest, most ordinary clothes they can find. ("Ordinary" is the root of the word "ornery.") There may be banners, slogans, ritual gestures and cries, and sometimes flags. The message is that we are many, we have taken over the street and are moving ahead, and we mean business.

Bibliography

The Drama Review. Special edition: *Processional Performance.* Vol. 29, Fall 1985.

Gary Jennings, *Parades! Celebrations and Circuses on the March.* Philadelphia and New York: J.B. Lippincott, 1966.

Walter Otto, *Dionysus: Myth and Cult.* Trans. Robert B. Palmer. Bloomington: Indiana University Press, 1965 (first published 1933).

BLUSH, CRINGE, FIDGET

*T*he reactions are physical all right: face turning red and sometimes white, voice switching to falsetto or to bass, stuttering, throat contracting, inhibited breath, dry mouth, stomach contractions, blinking, lowered head and eyes, shaking, fumbling, fidgeting, plucking at the clothes, hands cold and twisting together or held behind the back, smile fixed, feet frozen. These are symptoms of embarrassment, or dis-ease. They are brought on by entirely social and mental conditions, and they constitute proof positive that the human body reacts directly to the mind, even without reference to willpower or design.

To be embarrassed is to be disclosed, in public. Both factors are important: you must have something to hide first, and you must have an audience. Fall over your shoes as you get out of your solitary bed in the morning, and you may curse but you will not blush: embarrassment is about how you look in *other people's* eyes. (Extremely sensitive people might blush in private—but only when imagining that audience, which remains indispensable to the experience.)

The revelation of something we wanted to keep hidden explains the fingering of our clothes: we touch, tighten, and arrange, reassuring ourselves that the shell is still in place. Clothes cover what society has decreed shall be concealed; and a good many embarrassing moments involve clothes: lacking them, popping out of them, or wearing the wrong ones.

What we would like to hide is most often the truth about ourselves: the inexperience, incompetence, and ignorance that lie behind the bombastic or slick facade. To step forward before the expectant crowd with every sign of cool control, and then to fall flat on your face, is to produce embarrassment at nightmare level. The slip on the banana peel, the rug sliding out from under are concrete shorthand for the public fall from grandeur that everyone who is sane can recognize and remember. Failure to live up to expectations is another cause for embarrassment, both for you (provided you understand the extent of your inadequacy) and for everybody watching. The mountain heaves, as Horace put it, and all it brings forth is a mouse.

The word *embarrass* is from the Spanish *embarazar*, "to hinder by placing a bar or impediment in the way." It creates confusion, as when the march of a column of ants is broken up by a sudden interference—someone "putting

their foot in it," perhaps. (In dialects of French and Spanish the equivalents of this word are coarse terms for "to get
someone pregnant [*embarazada*].") Germans use the word
verlegen—to put something in the wrong place. The original sense of the French *gêne* is "confession." It came to
mean the torturing of someone, forcing them to own up;
and finally settled down to signify the peculiarly French
discomfort of embarrassment.

The specific meaning of *embarrassment* in English
arrives fairly late in the language. The term once meant
merely "not knowing what to do" in a specific situation,
for instance when confronted by a dilemma (as in the
French *embarras de choix*), or when there is a superfluity of
good things (an *embarras de richesses*). The narrowing of
this sense, till we get "an inability to respond where a
response is due," approaches the modern English meaning
of the word. One can still feel "financially embarrassed," or
unable to pay. The sense of inadequacy that having no
money can arouse in the breasts of upright citizens was
then further honed and differentiated until we get the
naming of the precise phenomenon we now call "embarrassment." It still includes occasions where we have to
respond but the role we must play is one we have not
learned. Examples are: finding yourself honoured by a surprise party, or having suddenly to dance in public (if you
are not in the habit of dancing, of course).

If, on the other hand, what your image *requires* is a
crowd of spectators, then, if no one takes any notice of

you, that absence will constitute your shame. If you set yourself up to give a speech and no one comes, the lack will hurt as much as being howled down. But even here, embarrassment comes about only if there are *some* people around: the three members who make up the audience, or the idle ticket sellers who watch you arrive, are needed in order for you to cringe. (Cringing is making yourself small, which is why embarrassment causes the hanging of heads, the shrinking back: these physically express the belittlement you see in the eyes of others.)

There is often complicity in the watching crowd; embarrassment is contagious. So when you step out on stage, or before the TV cameras, and start to sing, only to hear yourself warbling way out of tune, the audience will start to squirm and blush on your behalf. They imagine what it must be like to be you—and they can do it because somewhere in their lives they too have experienced your fate. It is far worse, of course, for members of the crowd who are your friends and relatives, for, as allies, their reputations are vested in your behaving "properly."

The only way socially to pass muster is to "fit in," as we say: to do what is proper, or "fitting." Impropriety, then, is the very stuff of embarrassment. Once again the body comes into play: exposure that is deemed "indecent" evokes embarrassment, and so do flatulence, snores, dribbles, burps, and sniffing. You should not be caught talking to yourself either, or picking your nose, or being smelly. To have committed such misdemeanours in public means the death of your reputation—and it is important to remember that in such cases whether you are to blame or not is of no significance. Your only hope is that the crowd, who usually have an interest in not interrupting the official agenda of the meeting, and in not being contaminated by an impropriety through drawing attention to it, will behave—at least for the moment—as though nothing has happened.

Incompetence is what impropriety of the embarrassing kind most often demonstrates. I once said to an important gentleman who arrived to visit my French landlady, "*Madame est sur le téléphone,*" and he answered gravely, "*Cela ne doit pas être très confortable.*" The stories travellers bring home from foreign countries often concern the embarrassing results of not knowing the language well enough, or not knowing what the social norms are: what you should on no account do or say. You bumble ahead with the best intentions, yet commit the offence—and the horror or the amusement you evoke cannot subsequently be put back into the bottle.

Involuntary impropriety is, of course, most acutely embarrassing when you cannot explain away what you have done. What you want more than anything else on earth is an escape from your predicament, and there is none. You are caught and helpless (which is why you wring or hide your hands in reaction to embarrassment). You haven't the vocabulary in the foreign language; or your situation is compromised in such a way that no one would believe your explanation if you have it, the clues pointing so much more plausibly to what the audience believes they can see. Into this category fall many of the cases of mistaken identity. You hug your husband, whisper extremely private endearments into his ear, then discover to your horror that you have made a mistake: this is not your husband at all. And immediately you know exactly what this total stranger must be thinking: sympathy is essential to embarrassment.

In spite of the great incompetence factor, the embarrassed reaction itself shows not that you lack social adjustment but that you have it, in spades. You *care* what society thinks, and really that is what it wants most. If we look at who most often gets embarrassed, we see that it is sensitive people, people who are trying hard to succeed, who are prepared to mend their ways, who never forget the lesson learned—and what more could society ask? On the whole, people who are never embarrassed (the "shameless") are the most antisocial of us, the least considerate and most uncaring.

The most exquisite kind of embarrassment, and the one that helps us see that the reaction need not merely mean a blind bowing to the pressures of convention, is the horrible realization that you might have hurt someone without intending to do so, or that your own arrogance has made you behave condescendingly where respect was due. Again you have demonstrated incompetence, but here the lesson learned has ethical implications.

Two women discuss, in Norwegian, the handicap of a man with one leg who is sitting opposite them on a Paris subway train. What would it be like to sleep with a one-legged man? The man gets up and says, in faultless Norwegian, "If you would care for a demonstration, Madam, I would be happy to oblige."

A friend of mine, invited by a Kurdish chieftain to a banquet in his mountain cave, decided to wear to the occasion a string of gold beads she had bought in the suq. She was especially proud of her good taste in having spotted and bought them, and decided to wear a little black dress to the feast, to show them off. When she was placed at the party among the women guests, she saw to her astonishment that every woman present was wearing the very same gold beads, but in abundance—massed in necklaces, bangles, and fringes, and sewn in profusion all over their clothes. The beads turned out to be traditional signs of dowry and wealth, of the esteem in which a man held his wife. She sat through the meal enduring the pity and concern of everyone present for her meagre lot in life.

My favourite example of this kind of embarrassment happened to John Fraser, the editor of *Saturday Night* magazine. Visiting one of Jean Vanier's l'Arche communities, he saw a man struggling with a carpentry chore, and spoke to him in a slow clear voice, with the nervously careful solicitude that we all reserve for the mentally retarded. He discovered later that the man was a Sorbonne professor who had taken time off to care for and learn from the handicapped. The way John tells this story, all those listening imagine themselves in the same position, being

kind. Then the punch line is delivered, to all of us. Embarrassment, when it is in working order, can produce enlight-
enment as well as shock.

Precisely because embarrassment often arises from
unawareness of important factors in the social environment, and because it is a powerful aid to learning and
never forgetting, it most commonly occurs in adolescence.
Almost all the good embarrassment stories happened when
we were young, and just discovering the mines and traps
laid for those who want desperately to find a place among
their peers. Very small children know fear and shyness, but
they never blush because of social faux pas.

Adults become surer and surer of themselves as well as
less and less sensitive, largely through knowing the rules,
and through practice and general wear and tear. It often
requires decades of experience and self-assurance before
the worst of our blunders can be told to other people. Yet
even then, what is laughing publicly at ourselves but further social complicity? We have found out not only that
everybody else knows what it's like to look a fool, but that
a very good way to defuse and rise above a crowd's contempt is to make an even larger crowd laugh *with* you,
even if it's at yourself.

Bibliography

Q. Horatius Flaccus, *De Arte Poetica* (ca. 20 BC), 139.

John Fraser, "Diary," *Saturday Night*. November 1988.

W.J. Froming et al., "The Influence of Public Self-Consciousness and the Audience's Characteristics on Withdrawal from Embarrassing Situations," *Journal of Personality* 58 (1990) 603–22.

Gabriele Taylor, *Pride, Shame, and Guilt: Emotions of Self-Assessment*. Oxford: Clarendon Press, 1985.

BELLS

*T*here is too much noise in a modern city for the sound of bells to be anything but incidental. Beepers, hooters, and sirens, themselves fighting to be heard over the roar of the traffic, have taken over many of the functions which bells fulfilled in the past. Church and clock towers are no longer the tallest buildings around: high-rise apartment dwellers next to a large tolling bell would risk being deafened by its din, so that fewer bells are allowed.

Most of us possess our own clocks, watches, radios, and televisions, so that we do not need to be communally reminded of the time, warned of disasters, or exhorted to rejoice, to mourn, or to pray by the sound of a bell. We have, however, considerably enlarged the repertoire of bells by adding them to bicycles and doors, and summoning each other to the telephone by means of repeated ringing: the ancient belief that names and fates are linked could find no stranger corroboration than the case of Alexander Graham Bell.

Pealing bells are superlative symbols still: easy to draw, visually expressive of both sound and movement, and further signifying (with the accompaniment of ribbons, leaves, and so on) joy, peace, togetherness, and cosmic harmony, with strong overtones of religion and nostalgia. No wonder bells are everywhere at Christmas—on cards, labels, signs, and decorations of every sort.

In many societies bells are an ancient institution. In China, bells have been known since at least 1030 BC; Indian women have worn ankle-bells for dancing for at least 4,000 years, and Hindu meditators often recollect themselves by the sound of a bell or a gong. The Koreans hang their magnificent bells close to the ground so that the vibration can sink into the earth, where hollow pots are buried to amplify the sound.

When Christians were first allowed to proclaim their religion openly in the fourth century, they chose a wooden board and hammer as a device for calling the faithful to church. Knocking had probably been a secret code long before; it made several Christian references, such as to the Cross, and to God's knocking for entrance to the human heart. Knocking on wood instead of ringing bells is still part of Holy Week solemnity in Spain and Portugal.

But bells, once embraced by Christianity, became one of its major signatures. Monasteries used them to mark times for prayer throughout the day and night, and soon the people living nearby came to depend on the sound for knowing what time it was. Eventually towns would have their own bells made, and use them to wake everybody up, open the markets, signal lunch-time, end work, close the city gates, and finally tell the townsfolk to cover their fires and retire for the night. (The word in French was *couvre-feu*, which becomes "curfew" in English.)

A man would stand at the top of the town's bell tower keeping watch at all times, and periodically ringing the bell to mark the hours. The name for this profession and this task is the origin of our term for the timepiece we now carry on our wrists. The Irish—who were among the first in the West to use the bell—called it *cloc*, which becomes German *Glocke*, French *cloche*, and English *clock*.

The vibration set up by bells has always made them objects of awe. Their ring has commonly been held to signify universal harmony—but Christians have maintained that the sound was not merely natural; it had something divine about it. In the late nineteenth century the sound was analysed and discovered indeed to be peculiar, and no more to be found in nature than is a cast bronze bell itself. There are five principal partial tones to a bell's ring: three notes in octave, one a perfect fifth, and the other (the one that gives bells their mysterious thrill) a minor third above the middle octave.

The Russians, whose tradition of bell-casting is a long and proud one, have always *chimed* their bells, that is, knocked a clapper tied to a rope against the bell's stationary sides. It is said that when, in an early movie, Russians first saw the Western method of ringing bells by agitating the entire bell instead of just the clapper inside, the audience broke up in gales of laughter at what seemed to them our monumentally stupid waste of effort.

Bells have often been treated with great affection, the largest and deepest of them especially being given names, like Big Ben, Great Tom, and Vienna's Pummerin, "the Growler." But cannons, like bells, are cast metal, and this has produced a nasty paradox in the West. Bells, which signify peace, have often been melted down to make weapons, as ploughshares used to be beaten into swords. Depriving people of their bells has long been a symbol of repression. The Nazis managed to seize and destroy 150,000 of Europe's bells to provide the metal for waging war.

Bibliography

John Camp, *Discovering Bells and Bellringing*. Aylesbury: Shire, 1975.

Percival Price, *Bells and Man*. Oxford University Press, 1983.

Jean-Pierre Rama, *Cloches de France et d'ailleurs*. Paris: Pierre Zech, 1993.

THE FEBRUARY FEAST

*O*n February 15 every year, goats were sacrificed and swiftly skinned. Their fresh and slithery hides were cut up into strips and tied round the hips of well-oiled but otherwise naked young men, who then ran round the track that traced the most ancient boundary of Rome. The runners carried more strips of goat-hide, with which they struck out at members of the watching crowd, especially women. The purpose of this ceremony was to purify (*februare*) the city; being hit by the thongs guaranteed fertility and easy childbirth. This was the origin of the name of the month, February.

The Christian version of the February feast pre-empted the date (celebrating it a day earlier) and substituted for the whole messy business a martyred saint, a sort of third-century heart-throb called Valentinus ("Strong Man").

Just before his death, the saint wrote a letter to his prison guard's blind daughter, and signed it "your Valentine." ("Valentine" originally meant the *sender* of the message, then its recipient [if willing], and later the card itself.)

The earliest surviving valentine was also written from prison: it is addressed by Charles, Duke of Orléans, to his family from the Tower of London, in 1415. Valentines are far older than Christmas cards, which have partly superseded them. They are a typically Anglo-Saxon and North American custom, though the tradition survives also in Germany and France.

Victorian England and nineteenth-century America saw the heyday of the valentine. First they had been hand-delivered as well as hand-written. After postal service was institutionalized came the invention and commercialization of printed, decorated cards with pre-written sentiments. Bought valentines quickly became extraordinarily elaborate: lacy, layered, patterned, embossed, multicoloured, padded, gilded, and impregnated with scent. Cards with moving paper figures were known as "mechanicals" or "sentimental movables." The earliest valentines and the most extravagant of them are collectors' pieces today.

The elaboration was not merely expressive of taste, but signalled new needs. Valentines had always been sent to friends and family as well as to lovers; it was the Victorians who began to lay renewed stress on the original sexual theme. Families were no longer arranging marriages the way they used to; young people had to find, approach, and "catch" their partners for themselves. Shyness and mystery became parts of the sender's role: through valentines you could express your love, prepare the ground as it were, before you dared actually to go public with it, and risk the embarrassment as well as the misery of a refusal.

Distance has always been important: the sender cannot, or pretends he cannot, approach the beloved directly. As the custom went into full swing, it became possible for women to send cards too—it was almost the only way they could admit their love, remaining protected by anonymity and distance. Puzzles and riddles allowed the loved one to guess at the lover's identity; they were also part of a far older oracular tradition, which clothed prophecies in riddling words and pointed to the chance-ridden and fateful aspect of love-matches.

The symbolism of valentines is still traditional: the passionate red heart struck by a wanton yet relentless Cupid with his arrow, shot from afar; birds, babies, and flowers referring to the fertile abundance of spring. (Birds were supposed to have found their mates and settled down to breed by February 14.) There are binding symbols: everlasting knots, rings, and hearts tied together.

Also, and more commonly these days, symbols represent not only tentativeness but merely temporary aspiration—people now expecting, even at this early stage, that love-matches will not last. Valentines are made of flimsy paper; gifts are candy and chocolate, soon consumed and forgotten.

Now that sexual approaches have become pat rather

than oblique, only about forty per cent of valentines are still sold to lovers. We have reverted to sending them also to family, friends, class-mates, colleagues: people to whom we ought to demonstrate benevolence.

Where valentines have spread to foreign cultures, new twists appear. In Japan, women give their men-folk chocolate shaped as "masculine" articles like ties and golf-balls. Because giving must evoke reciprocity in Japan, men give presents to women one month later: *white* chocolate this time, on the newly instituted festival known as White Day.

What used to be a minor tradition in valentines has grown much larger of late: that of jokes and rude messages. These used to be intended to tease old maids and unforthcoming bachelors out of remaining irritatingly single. Comical cards now include a whole new line openly intended for men, from women. They are familiar, tough, cynical, and peculiarly modern:

> You are always there when my luck runs out—
> You are always there when things go wrong—
> You are always there when I'm sad and blue—
> ARE YOU A JINX?

Another card has a pastel and soppy exterior, but once opened delivers a neat modern let-down: "Of all the people I've ever met ... you're one of them."

Bibliography

Elizabeth Andoh, "New Waves in Japanese Cooking: Cross-Cultural Currents," *The Journal of Gastronomy*, Spring 1989, p. 62.

Geoffrey Chaucer, "The Parlement of Foules," ca. 1392, in John H. Fisher, ed., *The Complete Poetry and Prose of Geoffrey Chaucer*. New York: Holt, Rinehart and Winston, 1977.

Dionysius of Halicarnassus, *Roman Antiquities*. From 7 BC. Vol. I., LXXX.

James George Frazer, *Appendix* to the Loeb edition of Ovid's *Fasti*. London: William Heinemann, 1967 (first published in 1931).

A.W.J. Holleman, *Pope Gelasius I and the Lupercalia*. Amsterdam: Adolf M. Hakkert, 1974.

A.L. Kellogg, "Chaucer's St Valentine: A Conjecture," in A.L. Kellogg, *Chaucer, Langland, Arthur: Essays in Middle English Literature*. New Brunswick: Rutgers University Press, 1972, pp. 108–45.

Henry Ansgar Kelly, *Chaucer and the Cult of Saint Valentine*. Leiden: E.J. Brill, 1986.

Ruth Webb Lee, *A History of Valentines*. New York: Studio Publications, 1952.

CAVIAR

*O*ne way of getting rid of the huge fish was to pile them up like cordwood on the beach and let the oil seep out of their bodies; you then set the whole heap alight. Each adult sturgeon was between three and six feet long, and could weigh over 200 pounds. In Canada in the 1850s they were worth about ten cents apiece—if you could find a buyer. It was hardly worth cutting them up, even for pig-feed. For one thing, sturgeon carry bony plates on the *outside* of their bodies. These, sharp and spiny in the young, tore up the fishing nets that were trying to bring up valuable whitefish and lake trout; the enormous adults, whose plates had worn smooth, just weighed everything down.

A great deal of hard work went into clearing North American lakes of sturgeon. People would spear them as they passed slowly under a bridge on their way to spawn;

they would drag a harpooned fish up by the rope, which would cause it nearly always to split or burst. The method was fairly effective, but unpleasant because of the eggs. The gravid females were absolutely crammed with eggs— about twenty-five pounds per fish. These would splatter all over the bridge, and soon begin to stink like hell.

Eggs rather like those are still to be found. Today, however, they travel, carefully refrigerated, all the way from Russia or Iran. During the 1980s, a small glass pot of them could cost about forty-five dollars—that's about fifteen dollars per teaspoon. And caviar, the roe of the sturgeon (no other fish gives real caviar), is still one of the most expensive foodstuffs in the world.

It is served up on sculpted ice, or in *présentoirs* of glass and silver with crushed-ice compartments. It should be eaten in solitary grandeur (never *ever* add *anything* to caviar, not even a drop of lemon juice) with a special long-handled spoon made of horn, mother-of-pearl, ivory, or gold. (Any metal other than gold ruins caviar.) A tiny piece of toast, upon which you lift the precious burden with your fingers, is permissible.

Always, caviar is accompanied by the metal lid which is its hallmark of authenticity. It is beluga, sevruga, or osetra, it comes from the Caspian Sea, and it is *malossol*, treated to "little salt." The only correct accompaniments are iced vodka (some recommend a bottle covered in moulded ice— a little slippery, one would have thought) or champagne: "To celebrate the sublime, summon only the perfect."

Caviar has always been greatly admired in Russia—as has the flesh of the sturgeon. The first fish and eggs of the season belonged to the Tsar. *Acipenser* (now its zoological name) was a noble fish in ancient Rome: it was served up adorned with wreaths, by slaves themselves crowned with greenery, and to the accompaniment of flutes. An unrepealed British law keeps sturgeon and whales, like swans, the perquisites of the monarch. The salted eggs, even when sturgeon abounded, were always the acquired taste of an élite: what most people could not appreciate was "caviar to the general." (In Shakespeare's day the word was both spelled and pronounced "cauiarie," with the accent on the first syllable.)

The real mystique of caviar (as opposed to sturgeon meat) began in the West only in 1920. It was invented by two Russo-Armenian brothers, Melkom and Mougcheg Petrossian, who had escaped to Paris during the Revolution. Realizing that caviar was not to be had in their new country, they simply telephoned Moscow and demanded some. They also asked for commercial rights to sixty-three per cent of Russian caviar exports—a privilege the family still enjoys.

At the Gastronomic Exhibition at the Grand Palais in 1920, Melkom and Mougcheg gave free tastings—and provided large pans for spitting out what most of the uninitiated could not stomach. It was a huge success: crowds came to watch the grimaces, cheer on the brave, and marvel at the rapturous few and at the price they were prepared to pay for salted fish eggs. The slot that many societies keep for one outrageously overvalued foodstuff was filled. Caviar is expensive, fabled, exotic, difficult to prepare, to keep, to transport, and to eat. It is also increasingly rare. The combination is irresistible.

The race of sturgeon, one of the great armoured fishes of the upper Cretaceous, survived in enormous numbers for over a hundred million years—until the mid-nineteenth century. The sturgeon is a scavenger on lake bottoms; it has no natural enemies. But the fact is that the wanton destruction of sturgeon by our ancestors looks benign when set beside the damage being done to them at present. In North America the few remaining sturgeon are threatened by the contaminated sediment that drains into lakes and rivers and settles there, increasingly blanketing their feeding grounds and killing off the crabs and clams they eat. The Caspian Sea itself is sinking because of dams, and pollution is tainting its waters.

We all see the need to save the sturgeon: North America has actually set up committees to discuss the remaining stocks. It would be a pity to waste those gold and ivory teaspoons. We could always, of course, reduce something else to rarity instead.

Bibliography

Athenaeus, *The Deipnosophists* (Second to third century AD.), Book vii, 294f.

Susan R. Friedland, *Caviar*. New York: Charles Scribner's Sons, 1986.

Horst Gödecken, *Le Caviar*. Marseille: Jeanne Laffitte, 1986.

William Shakespeare, *Hamlet*. Act II, scene ii, l. 447.

J.W. Spooner and F.A. MacDougall, *The Lake Sturgeon*. Ontario Department of Lands and Forests, Fish and Wildlife Branch, 1961.

Maguelonne Toussaint-Samat, *Histoire naturelle et morale de la nourriture*. Paris: Bordas, 1987, pp. 283–90.

THE PROFESSIONALS

*M*embers of the professions make up the modern world's version of an aristocratic class. We constantly praise and propitiate professionals by offering them large sums of money, together with trembling respect and fear. The clients of professionals make themselves utterly vulnerable to them; and no one can really be called a professional unless he or she is officially placed in a position to do direct, personal damage to a client.

The world's oldest profession is the priesthood, and upon it all the others are modelled. There are still only three other professions in the fullest and strictest sense: the law, medicine, and university professorship. Groups like architects, engineers, and psychologists are closing in, with some success, upon the central group of four.

It is the public that really decides who is professional, because it is we who have to do the trusting. We do not grant total obeisance to school teachers, although we entrust our children to them, because we think we know as much as they do. Librarians are not dangerous enough, and we think of them as knowing only where books are, not what is in them. We have not yet fully understood that architects can spoil our lives even if their buildings do not fall down; and anyway we never meet them face to face. Pharmacists are given orders by doctors, and professionals must be autonomous; the military are dangerous all right, but also under orders.

The anachronistic component of honour which is granted by society to professionals requires them (partly, perhaps, out of revenge) to be seen to suffer in order to get where they are. They must undergo long preparatory years of study, followed by examinations that are designed to be proofs of stamina as much as prowess. Professionals then band themselves into secretive fellowships which protect their members and work hard on excluding outsiders.

The initiation of adepts into these groups may be effected by the bestowal of symbolic objects: of beribboned documents, of iron rings for engineers, of significantly coloured hoods for university professors. Professionals may go on to distinguish themselves by wearing special clothes: white coats, greenish wrappers and face-masks, wigs, mortarboards, scapulars, hoods, dog-collars, and black cloaks.

They keep their numbers down so that the value of

those professing remains as high as possible, and they fight off pretenders to the fold. Because there are so few of them, professionals have very little time. One physical demonstration of their power is the sight of numbers of us crowded onto chairs round the walls of waiting-rooms, waiting. They have no time to do the "dirty work," like cleaning up, or preparing documents, or marking routine tests, or even welcoming and readying clients for their attentions; other people—non-professionals—are paid less to do this for them.

What makes people professional is their arcane knowledge. No one else knows what they know; it follows that no one can judge them but the small group of their peers, the other initiates. They judge themselves; and we all helplessly know that professionals, grouped together in brotherhoods, look out most especially for their membership. They might refer, for questions of moral responsibility, to a "code of ethics"— the very existence of which reminds us all of the danger they could pose.

One definition of a professional, in sport or in art for example, is that he or she is paid for work done: payment, in our society, proves value. But it is exceedingly important for professional mystique that they *do not work for money*. They have a "calling," a "gift," a love for their work in and for itself. Members of the four "full" professions are distinguished by their access to the client at his or her most personal, private, and vulnerable. Yet their attitude must remain utterly impersonal. Professionals are interested in

Torts or in Italian Renaissance Lyric or in Intestinal Block-
ages, not in you yourself. We loathe this about professionals, but we also dread personal entanglements with them,
because they could so easily abuse our trust. Professionals
have to keep secrets: they know, they could tell—but of
course they won't, will they? They judge whether you are
capable or not—and their judgement is impartial and just,
isn't it?

Modern democratic society does everything it can to
reduce the power of the professions. It tries to call as many
people as possible "professionals"; and indeed the original
professionals have been so successful in obtaining excellent working conditions for themselves that everyone in
our society not only longs but fights to get the same perks,
even if we cannot achieve the same high pay. Consumers
of professional services keep professionals under constant
surveillance and threat of legal sanction. The state tries to
make them accept wages, or to control their fees; it
attempts to decide where and under what conditions professionals will work. But *how* they do what they do remains
impossible to govern.

We hate needing these people, but the conviction
among us is strong that although they are few, rich, organized, and dangerous, they are also irreplaceable and indispensable. We had better just get on with trusting them. If
we honour them enough they might turn out to be honourable, mightn't they?

Bibliography

T.S. Chivers, "The Proletarianisation of a Service Worker," *Sociological Review* 21 (1973) 633–55.

(Editorial staff), "Professions libérales: l'heure du renouveau," *L'Express*, 8 novembre 1985, 36–43.

William J. Goode, "The Theoretical Limits to Professionalization," in Amitai Etzioni, ed., *The Semi-Professions and Their Organization*. New York: Free Press, 1969, pp. 266–313.

J.M. Gustafson, "Professions as 'Callings,'" *The Social Service Review* 56 (1982) 501–15.

Bruce A. Kimball, *The "True Professional Ideal" in America: A History*. Cambridge, MA, and Oxford, U.K.: Blackwell, 1992.

Harold Perkin, *The Rise of Professional Society: England since 1880*. London: Routledge, 1990.

William Joseph Reader, *Professional Men: The Rise of the Professional Classes in Nineteenth-Century England*. London: Weidenfeld and Nicolson, 1966.

Harold L. Wilensky, "The Professionalization of Everyone?" *The American Journal of Sociology* 70 (1964) 137–58.

THE LEFT HAND

*T*he human body is less symmetrical than it looks. Internally, our organs are not divided neatly down the middle—the heart, for example, being both inclined and on the left—and externally our hands are almost invariably quite unequal, although they apparently mirror each other. About ninety per cent of people are right-handed; the other ten per cent have a strong preference for the left. This is one of our differences from animals, among whom fifty per cent prefer the right front leg, fifty per cent prefer the left, and ambidextrous behaviour is far more common than in human beings.

Body images are among the most powerful metaphors we have; "culture" seizes upon the body and uses it to express moral ideas, social structures, prejudices, preferences, fears, and ideals. Often the metaphor squeezes the facts into its own mould: the "heart" of anything is its middle, even though our hearts are definitely off-centre. We have always emphasized the difference in efficiency between our two hands; we have then meditated on the weakness of the left, and used it to confirm our worst suspicions.

The right hand, in almost every language and every culture on earth, means permanence, reliability ("a right-hand man"), power, truth, and rectitude. Dexterity, acceptability, immediacy, and correctness are "right-handed" in English; "sinister" means "left," a word that itself derives from Anglo-Saxon *lyft*: "weak" or "worthless." *Droit* in French is "straight" and also "just," while someone *gauche* ("gawky" in English) is maladroit. An Italian who is *mancino* is left-handed—or treacherous. In many cultures dealings with the dead are carried out with the left hand, since its connotations are with the dark, the inept, the polluted, the obstinately unknowable. Leftness is commonly used to express whatever is outside the official life of the group.

Women have tended everywhere to be classified as "left." The feeling behind this is that they are irrational, lower (most people gesture with the right hand for "high" and "front", and with the left for "low" and "behind"), dark, marginal, fluid, cold, deceitful, and generally sinister. Men (on the other hand) are high, dry, straightforward, lucid, bright—and right.

On the continent of Europe, couples when marrying give each other rings, a custom that is spreading as equality strengthens between the sexes. Among post-Reformation Anglo-Saxons, only the woman has traditionally worn the ring, on the fourth finger of the left or "female" hand. The "ring" or "gold" finger was believed to have a direct arterial connection with the left-leaning, passionate, irrational, but—one hoped—faithful heart.

Left-handed people have always been pressured by the majority to conform. Even when not forced by anxious parents and misguided educators to use the less capable hand, they have had for example to shake hands with the right because other people do it, or to use tools constructed for right-handers.

More men than women are in fact left-handed. In the ancient world they had worse difficulties than we, because it mattered desperately in battle that your shield arm covered your heart, while the other did the fighting; and for a member of a phalanx to insist on wielding his sword in the left would have meant leaving a chink in the wall of overlapping shields, and jeopardizing the safety of the whole troop.

In many societies where eating is done with the hands, the left hand is disqualified as profane, and kept for polluting and unpleasant tasks deemed beneath the dignity of the right. Greek and Roman diners put left hands out of commission by leaning on their left elbows as they reclined at meals, and eating with the right. A left-hander attempting to use his more capable hand would find himself lying down the wrong way round; unless he conformed he could ruin the configuration of the party.

Modern science has shown us that the right hand has usually been governed by the *left* side of the brain all along—and vice versa. Speech, even in most left-handers, is a function mainly of the left brain. The right half of the brain has become the subject recently of much attention and speculation: it is as large, as complex, as the left half, but we are far less certain what it does, apart from its evident governance over perceptions of space, including the ability to recognize faces.

"Left" and "right" have lost some of their force as metaphors, as the strength ebbs from the prejudice against women which they used to express. But left- and right-handedness have acquired a powerful new fascination: they are now recognized as clues, the full significance of which remains mysterious, to the workings of the human brain.

Bibliography

H. Hécaen and J. de Ajuriaguerra, *Left-Handedness: Manual Superiority and Cerebral Dominance.* New York: Grune and Stratton, 1964.

Robert Hertz, *Death and The Right Hand.* Trans. Rodney and Claudia Needham. Glencoe, Ill.: Free Press, 1960 (originally published 1915).

William Jones, *Finger-Ring Lore.* London: Chatto and Windus, 1877.

John Russell Napier, *Hands.* London: Allen and Unwin, 1980.

Rodney Needham, ed., *Right and Left.* University of Chicago Press, 1973.

Sally P. Springer and Georg Deutsch, *Left Brain, Right Brain.* New York: W.H. Freeman and Co., 1989.

WEDDING CAKE

*W*eddings revolve around brides. Wearing her extraordinary clothes, flanked by "maids" in costume, waited upon, stared at, toasted, envied, and admired, a woman who becomes "the bride" for a day must necessarily steal the show. Even the groom is merely a bridegroom ("the bride's man"), and in the past in Britain there were also the bride bed, the bride ale, many small cakes, and finally a single large one called "the bride cake." Its name changed to "wedding cake" during the nineteenth century.

A bride cake was round, flat like an oatcake, and spiced. An early custom was, after the ritual of the ring, to break the cake over the bride's head. This invoked fertility, as where brides in several different cultures are showered with rice, "many small things," signifying a fecund future.

Breaking the cake was also figurative of the end of the bride's maidenhead.

Modern wedding cakes in the Anglo-Saxon tradition are not designed to maintain this ritual. They are huge and gorgeous creations, one of the major expenses of a "white" wedding. A wedding cake may be piped with scrolls, scattered with icing flowers, studded with pearls and silver balls, beribboned, caged in a shiny sugar filigree, and topped with a nosegay of fresh flowers or porcelain figurines of the bride and her groom.

Wedding cakes mount in tiers, cake upon cake; they can reach a height of eight feet, and even sport a fountain at the top, made to descend, without wetting the cake, via aqueducts to a pumping device that forces the water up to fall again. The top tier of the cake (the littlest one) may be kept for the christening party of the couple's first child, or to celebrate the first anniversary of the wedding: fruitcakes can be expected, with care, to last a year. Americans prefer sponges, even cheesecakes, which are light and resolutely ephemeral.

The English cake derives from three main traditions: the ancient plum pudding or dried fruit concoction symbolic of festive plenty; the small almond-paste, iced "marchpanes" of the Renaissance, which gave us the distinctive double icing; and the medieval "subtlety." "Subtleties" were bravura pieces, created to surprise and delight noble guests. They were served at banquets as a form of entertainment, and included such fantasies as sugar sculptures, and four and twenty blackbirds baked in a pie. (Stag parties are said still to boast of ladies leaping out of cardboard cakes.)

Our wedding cakes are almost the last of the great culinary pyramids and constructions that used to be in such demand at feasts. Since the early twentieth century in Britain, the tiers have been lifted on pillars. (Upturned champagne-glasses are now a popular variant.) Americans prefer sugar fondant to almond paste, and cakes that maintain the older ziggurat form because soft cake cannot support pillars. Upper layers of soft cake are held up by a system of wooden dowels and cardboard plateaux disguised with piped icing or ribbon. Canadians participate in both traditions. The fruitcake group often insist on making their own layers from a family recipe, bringing the results to be mounted on pillars and iced by professionals.

The bride can share her luck by tossing her bouquet or giving guests bits of her cake. Girls used to take these home and sleep with them under their pillows to induce dreams of future husbands. The sharing of the cake now tends to be honed severely, to save time. The bottom layer is often all the cake there is, serving only as matter for the first ritual cut, and, in America, the sharing of the first slice between bride and groom; the other layers are made of iced styrofoam. Sometimes the whole edifice is fake; ready-sliced and even boxed bits of real cake are brought separately and handed out to guests. We should "not even discuss" putting wedding cake under our pillows, according to one master confectioner— hers admittedly being of the *génoise* and cheesecake variety.

But there is no wedding without photographs of the bride and groom together Cutting the Cake. The custom spread in the 1930s, when dense British cakes were encased in extra-hard white icing, to hold up the pillared layers. Grooms "helped" brides to cut the cake with a beribboned knife or sword. Now the pair perform as a team. The cake stands tall, white, archaic and decorated, pyramidal like the veiled bride herself, and dominating the proceedings; it is a version of the bride, and the piercing of it dramatizes her rite of passage.

Bibliography

Margaret Baker, *Wedding Customs and Folklore*. Newton Abbot: David and Charles, 1977.

Rose Levy Beranbaum, *The Cake Bible*. New York: William Morrow, 1988.

Simon R. Charsley, "Interpretation and Custom: The Case of the Wedding Cake," *Man* 22 (1987) 93–110.

Simon R. Charsley, "The Wedding Cake: History and Meanings," *Folklore* 99 (1988) 232–41.

Simon R. Charsley, *Wedding Cakes and Cultural History*. London and New York: Routledge, 1992.

John Cordy Jeaffreson, *Brides and Bridals*. (2 vols.) London: Hurst and Blackett, Vol. I, 1872.

TAKING A SHOWER

*W*hen showers began to be promoted in Europe in the mid-nineteenth century, they were cold, and believed to be dangerous if not managed correctly. But they had the advantage of being cheap. People might submit to them because their betters had decided they needed a wash: prisons and armies enforced rules such as "a shower once a fortnight, a foot-bath once a week." Files of unwilling bodies were firmly marched under jets of icy water, directed by men standing on ladders. With eight being doused simultaneously, about a hundred could be washed in one hour with no more water than that required to fill eight bathtubs.

But douches, in the hands of the experts, could equally well become "water cures," in which sprays were aimed at those parts of the body requiring healing. The problem was always water pressure. Some hydropathic establishments installed a high water tank beneath which a patient stood for a "regenerative" shower. A valve opened at the pull of a cord and let the water fall. Patients had to wear hard hats to protect their heads.

Shower-takers also attempted the difficult task of keeping their feet dry, for this was thought to lessen the shock. One stood stooped forward on a *dry* carpeted stool in a shallow round tub or hip bath. A tank of water, of the same volume as the tub or less, was supported on a tripod over one's head. First the water had to be hand-pumped from a bucket up a pipe and into the tank. Then, after mustering courage, one tugged a chain, and the water descended.

Devices that sprayed rather than doused people were known at first as rain baths; one of these was the "shower bath ring" in which a perforated tube was worn round the neck and water supplied to it by a pipe leading from the bath tap: in this manner a bather could be surrounded by a private rain storm, while keeping the head dry. Showers have until very recently been a mainly male choice, tough and swift, forceful and athletic; women have tended to engage in longer, gentler grooming rituals, which typically included bath-tub soaking.

Cold showers were frequently taken after hot baths, by people rich enough to command a hot bath, for the sake of health rather than of cleanliness. Ever since Homeric times, warm baths have been a sign, in the West, of "soft," luxurious, and therefore slightly wicked living. It has often

been felt that cold water ought to suffice, and that habitu-
ating oneself to cold water might build character. Hot
baths were often thought therefore to *require* cold showers
afterwards, to "close the pores" of the skin and put an end
to too much hedonism. (People will put up with a cold
shower where they draw the line at a cold bath.)

Lying in a hot bath used to be one of the ways in which
one warmed up in a mostly unheated house. For showering
all year round in cold climates to become popular, we
required not only the arrival of water pipes at all houses
and water pressure strong enough to drive water automatically up to the shower head, but also water heaters and central heating. In most places, the fashion for habitual
showering has really arrived only within the last forty years.

Baths have now become comparatively old-fashioned.
Many of us never use a bathtub except as somewhere to
stand when showering. Lying down in hot water is time-
consuming, peaceful, and passive. (In our family one "has"
a bath but "takes" a shower.) Showers, now routinely used
by women as well as men, are brisk, active, and thought of
as quick—though many people, especially the young, are
reputed to stand for longer and longer periods of time
under the shower.

Though most of us are quite clean to start with, we feel
that bathing means sitting in our own dirty water, whereas
showers carry the dirt straight off and down the plug-hole.
The preference for showering over bathing has resulted in
a small but definite change in behaviour: where once we

used to fill a basin of water in order to wash our hands, we are now more likely to soap them under a running tap.

People wash their hair more often today than they have ever done in history. The recent invention of extra-gentle shampoo is the reason we can do this almost every day without damaging our scalps, and showers both encourage the habit and are demanded by it. Shower caps have meanwhile gone to live with hair rollers.

Many of us cannot imagine leaving the house without a shower; others shower in the evening, dispelling the grime and unpleasantness of the working day. Modern life is founded on an enormous opposition between the public and private realms of every human life. Showers have become rituals of passage for us, from one realm to the other. They reassure us that we are not grubby or smelly, and are therefore either restored to privacy or acceptable in public. They purify us as aspersions of water always have done in religious ritual; they "make us feel good."

Bibliography

Richard L. Bushman and Claudia L. Bushman, "The Early History of Cleanliness in America," *Journal of American History* 74 (1988) 1213–38.

Homer, *Odyssey*. Eighth century BC. 8, 248–49; 10, 358–74.

M. Langford, *Personal Hygiene: Attitudes and Practices*. Ithaca: Cornell University Agricultural Experiment Station, New York State College of Home Economics, 1965.

Ellen Lupton and J. Abbott Miller, *The Bathroom, the Kitchen and the Aesthetics of Waste: A Process of Elimination*. Princeton Architectural Press, for the M.I.T. List Visual Arts Center, 1992.

Georges Vigarello, *Concepts of Cleanliness: Changing Attitudes in France since the Middle Ages*. Trans. Jean Birrell. Cambridge University Press, 1988.

Lawrence Wright, *Clean and Decent*. Revised edition with Dave Larder. London and Boston: Routledge and Kegan Paul, 1980 (originally published 1960).

CROSSWORD PUZZLES

$\mathcal{E}$ ver since mastery of speech proved we were human, people have loved mind-stretching word puzzles: questions like "What is it that walks on four legs in the morning...?" or meaning-laden names, as in "Thou art Peter and upon this rock...." To all the double-entendres constructed of pure sound, written letters have added acrostics (letters in the verses of a poem which, read vertically, make a word), palindromes (phrases that read the same backwards and forwards, like the one with which Adam introduced himself to Eve: MADAM, I'M ADAM), anagrams (convert JAMES STUART, and get A JUST MASTER), and homomorphs (as when SEWER can mean a needle, not a drain).

Crossword-puzzle addicts are people obsessed with language. Many of them love filling in a grid with letters that make up words answering simple definitions. Others are a more twisted breed altogether: having understood that words are patterns which can be reshaped and reinterpreted, they cannot resist playing about with that fearsome power. There are now more than fifty million regular cruciverbalists, representing every alphabetically written language on earth. Yet the form of this particular word mania, ancient as are its roots, was set only in 1913, when Arthur Wynne printed a clued and numbered "Word-cross," in the shape of a diamond with a blank centre in the form of a cross, in the Christmas edition of the Sunday *New York World.*

In 1924 the first crossword puzzle book was published, and the craze took off. That same year crosswords arrived in England, where the cryptic version of the puzzle would soon emerge, with its riddles, its poetry, and its compilers' rules ("Always say what you mean, though you don't always mean what you say"). By the 1940s, crosswords were known to be so irresistible in Britain that in January 1945 the Nazis scattered propaganda puzzles in English from a buzz-bomb. A typical clue: "We hear that this is a rare commodity in England (3)" (EGG). In the Soviet Union, magazine readers were invited to "unravel" even more blatant, politically correct messages, such as "American puppet in Bonn circus (8)" (ADENAUER).

The puzzle's popularity has never abated since it became a world-wide obsession in the twenties. For those who like them, crosswords can absorbingly fill in the time we spend in waiting rooms, lining up, commuting, travelling, or unwinding after stressful work that leaves the brain stimulated but hungry. Only puzzle, pencil, and solver are required. Great stretches of our lives, especially our waiting hours, are lived alone these days, and crosswords are solitary pursuits.

They are perfect examples of "closed system" thinking, the chief strategies of which are extrapolation and interpolation. This type of thinking is different from much scientific, artistic, and even everyday discursive thought; it requires logic, memory, and a particular kind of agility and tenacity of mind. A person with a combination of such characteristics delights in carefully framed occasions for setting them all in operation.

Sometimes puzzlers are rewarded with flashes of insight, when they "just know" a solution to a cryptic clue, even before they consciously understand the reasoning; it is an exciting and satisfying sensation. Solving at record speed, in the intense competitions which are now common, requires a large dose of this ability to leap over the intervening (but always present) logical steps. (Eight and a half minutes has been clocked for *The Times* of London's contest; the record set at three and a half minutes in 1970 still stands—but the puzzle became much more difficult soon after that date.)

What is "cut and run" in seven letters? (OPERATE.) Leather moved from side to side, by the sound of it (5)? (SUEDE.) What makes dat guy's appearance no longer dat guy's (8)? (DISGUISE.) Crosswords love abbreviations (L is left, V is five), and conventions like "the French" (LE, LA, LES), O for "love," or PP, "very soft." Crossword country is full of tors and heather (ling), and overrun with emus, asps, lions, imps, saints (ST, SS), and people with Old Testament names (Eli, Amos, and Eve). Cryptic clues may involve puns, allusions, anagrams, hidden words, ambiguous definitions, charades, reversals, rebuses, deletions, containers, combinations: solvers must spot which tricks are being played before they can see through them.

The compiler is the unseen fiend with whom they do battle. Some of these trap-setters have achieved immortality, like the great Torquemada (Edward Powys Mathers) of the *Observer*, who would sit cross-legged on his bed "very like a somewhat relaxed Buddha," smoking and gazing into the distance until something clicked, whereupon, "with a contented smile or discontented shrug," he wrote down his clue. (His wife performed the more mundane but possibly even more difficult task of constructing the grid, with words he supplied.)

Torquemada once devised a "Knock-knock.—Who's there?" crossword, made up of clues like "Blank fool and caught a cold (8)": ABINADAB. Afrit of *The Listener* made a grid in which his own face lurked, with Q's for eyes. Compilers with minds like these rejoice in demonic pseudonyms: Mephisto and Afrit (A.F. Ritchie) are both devils, while Torquemada, Ximenes, and Azed (reversed) were leaders of the Spanish Inquisition.

Bibliography

Tony Augarde, "Crosswords," in *The Oxford Guide to Word Games*. New York: Oxford University Press, 1984.

Sir Frederic Charles Bartlett, *Thinking: An Experimental and Social Study*. London: Allen and Unwin, 1958 (esp. pp. 63–66).

Roger Millington, *Crossword Puzzles: Their History and Cult*. London: Nelson, 1974.

Colin Parsons, *How to Solve a Crossword*. London: Hodder and Stoughton, 1988.

SITTING PRETTY

*W*hen people decide to avoid sitting on the ground, and place three- or four-legged supports beneath their buttocks instead, they are choosing to limit and constrain their behaviour in important ways. Chairs force us to sit where they are placed and, if we habitually use them, quite early in our lives they reduce the ability of our muscles to encompass the postures required for floor-sitting. A typical, healthy, middle-aged person living in a modern western culture must expect to suffer agonies if forced to live even a few weeks without the use of any chair.

Floor-sitters never learn to need back-support, or to be unable to squat; their knees, their hip-joints, their ankles retain the suppleness which they—and we—had when babies. Travelling Americans and Europeans, encountering it in adults, have often thought such versatility highly improper.

"They reminded one," wrote Commodore Perry of the U.S. Navy when visiting the Japanese in 1853, "of those skillful contortionists or clowns, who exhibit their caoutchouc accomplishments to the wonderment of the spectators."

Anthropologists have enumerated at least 132 ways of sitting, only about thirty of which involve anything comparable with a chair; and of these many are thought, even now and even for men, to be unbecoming in our own polite society. Women should strictly speaking use only very few sitting positions, with legs either together or crossed; crossing their legs at the knee represented a revolutionary relaxation of the norms in quite recent times.

The constricting and formalizing effect of chairs on human posture has made them symbols of status from the beginning; comfort was a consideration which counted far less, until as late as the nineteenth century. A throne, for instance, is a special decorated chair, often the only chair in the "throne room." Its occupant is not only isolated and made easily visible to everyone, but "raised" in metaphorical ways as well. He or she must sit upright and impressively still: rigidity and immobility are often essential components of decorum. Because sitting on a chair means dignity (we show deference, in our culture, by standing in the presence of another), inviting a guest to sit on a chair is an ancient and powerful gesture of hospitality and respect.

Chairs mean that eating and writing tables must be raised too, waist-high so that legs can fit under them. Specialization of function is typical of chairs: they have different appearances and statuses, and are kept in different places, depending on whether they are kitchen, drawing-room, dining-room, or garden chairs; then there are variants such as settees, love-seats, rockers, highchairs, and chaises-longues.

The living spaces of floor-sitters are far less formally differentiated than ours have become. All human societies limit the number of bodily postures that count as proper, but floor-sitters, especially males, usually have a broader repertoire than we permit.

People who live without chairs (the chairless and the chaired almost invariably inhabit different worlds) are accustomed from childhood to seeing everything in the house from lower down. The great film director Yasujiro Ozu created his striking, intensely Japanese style partly through placing his camera, for interior scenes, as low as the eye-level of someone kneeling on the floor, so that the audience sees everything from the point of view from which traditional Japanese were accustomed to seeing.

The floors in chairless rooms must be warm (made from wood, for instance, rather than stone) and kept meticulously clean. The people who live in them do not normally wear boots or laced shoes, because footwear is removed on entering a house where people sit on the floor, and must be easy to put on and take off. Their clothes are flowing and long, if much clothing be worn at all.

Our own clothing is designed with chairs very much in mind. The most "liberated" miniskirted woman in nylon stockings is peremptorily forbidden the floor, even if she should be capable of sitting for hours with her ankles on the same level as her sitting bones and without leaning on anything. Men's pants are quickly ruined and usually become uncomfortable if worn on the floor.

It is believed that the Chinese, who adopted chairs in the eleventh century AD, did so because chairs, like raised beds, lifted people out of the reach of draughts. They already knew the folding stool, an exotic import which they called *hu ch'uang*, literally "barbarian bed," because of its legs. After the adoption of rigid chairs, *yi* (from a root word meaning "to lean"), the Chinese changed their costume, for example to include trousers. However, they continued to speak of mats in contexts where they now mean chairs: Chairman Mao, for instance, translates literally as Mat-Master Mao.

Bibliography

Charles Patrick Fitzgerald, *Barbarian Beds: The Origin of the Chair in China*. London: Cresset Press, 1965.

John Gloag, *The Chair: Its Origins, Design, and Social History*. South Brunswick, N.J., and New York: A.S. Barnes, 1964.

Gordon Winant Hewes, "World Distribution of Certain Postural Habits," *American Anthropologist* 57 (1955) 231–44.

Matthew Calbraith Perry, *Narrative of the expedition of an American squadron to the China seas and Japan, under the command of Commodore M.C. Perry, United States Navy*. London: Macdonald, 1954, p. 158.

Donald Richie, *Ozu*. Berkeley: University of California Press, 1974.

Bernard Rudofsky, *Now I Lay Me Down to Eat*. Garden City, New York: Anchor Books, 1980, Chapter 2.

GLOVES

*G*loves, in German, are called "hand shoes." Like shoes, they evolved as a protection for the extremities. But their quirky, unmistakable shape, and their manner of taking on individual bodily idiosyncrasies so that they seem eerily part of the person even when they are off, have assured for gloves, as for shoes, a rich social and psychological significance. Fingerless mittens—either the simple bags with thumbs, or the ones that leave the fingers protruding—used to be thought appropriate for children, old people, and those who merely wished to keep their hands warm. Fingers were what made gloves in the past suggestive of authority and prestige; lower-class people were sometimes forbidden to wear gloves with fingers.

The elasticity of fine thin leather such as kid was prized before stretch fabrics or glove sizes were invented. Aristocratic hands covered with pale kid gloves looked smooth, costly, narrow, and manifestly unacquainted with work. Men and women would go to bed wearing gloves filled with cream, to whiten and soften their hands. Eighteenth-century Irish "chickenskin" gloves were even thinner and smoother than kid. They were cut from the skins of aborted calves, and so fine that they came folded into the shell of a walnut.

Long narrow glove fingers had to be eased open with wooden stretchers before they could be put on. They were commonly made as much as two centimetres longer than any normal finger, and stitching was continued on the outside of the glove as far as the knuckles, to make fingers look as lengthy and as tapering as possible; they were the equivalents of pointed toes on shoes. Glovers combined their trade with that of perfumery, and the best leather gloves were scented with musk, civet, ambergris, and spirit of roses.

The immensely complex symbolism of gloves derives, of course, from the meanings of hands. As with a hand-shake, gloves meant faith and confidence: investitures or the transference of property could be symbolized by handing over a glove. They were pledges of protection and authority, as when the king's glove was erected on a pole during a free fair. They signified honour and courage: flinging down a gauntlet was a challenge and a demand for satisfaction, if necessary by trial of strength.

Gloves were gifts always acceptable to and indeed expected by important people: they expressed the giver's loyalty and esteem. They were also given to workers to secure their goodwill when a big job was begun, to guests at weddings and at funerals, and to recipients of favour on St Valentine's Day. Gloves "lined" with money were famous as formal bribes. High-up people often received, on symbolic occasions, far too many pairs of gloves to use them all; for this reason, fine specimens survive in large numbers for the pleasure of collectors. These are often jewelled, beaded, fringed, embroidered, and masterfully cut and sewn.

The etiquette of glove-wearing was based on ideas of power attaching to whether a glove was on (generally, in the declining of physical contact with others, a sign of superiority); or off (a token of respect). It was often correct, for instance, for a man to remove his glove to shake hands, whereas a woman kept hers on—she being both ritually superior and modest. Two equals or two intimates both took their gloves off. Servants kept gloves on so they would touch no-one directly; pristine white gloves for waiters were proof, in addition, that fingers had not slipped into the sauce.

Elegant *convives* took gloves off for dinner—no mean feat this, for women who wore buttoned kid reaching to their elbows or above. The gloves were then somehow to be kept from slithering off satin laps at the table. Carrying them has always been a nuisance. Children's mittens are prudently tied together with a long string that passes down the sleeves of the wearers' jackets, so that mitts can dangle at the ready when taken off. The shoulder-tabs often thought to be a smart finishing touch on blouses were originally placed on soldiers' and doormen's jackets, for buttoning down over temporarily unneeded gloves.

Only a few decades ago it was considered polite, especially for women, to put on gloves whenever leaving the house: they were formal fashion accessories, and hands were to be exposed only in private. Nowadays, we are utilitarian about gloves as about most things. An aura of moneyed competence still clings, however, to sporting gloves: to hand-coverings for driving, golfing, and bicycling. Baseball mitts and mighty hockey and boxing gloves are cunningly designed, carefully regulated, tough, purposeful, and fearsomely specific. The people who wear these know what they are doing; their gloves are there to protect their hands, yes—but also to proclaim their prowess to those of us who merely clap.

Bibliography

S.W. Beck, *Gloves, Their Annals and Associations: A Chapter of Trade and Social History.* London: Hamilton, Adams, 1883.

Pearl Binder, *The Peacock's Tail.* London: Harrap, 1958.

Valerie Cumming, *Gloves.* London: Batsford, 1982.

B.E. Ellis, *Gloves and the Glove Trade.* London: Isaac Pitman, 1921.

Joan Wildeblood, *The Polite World: A Guide to the Deportment of the English in Former Times.* Revised ed. London: Davis-Poynter, 1973.

THE FIREPLACE

*T*he Latin word for "fireplace" is *focus*. The English meaning of "focus" has developed directly from the functions of the hearth. People once cooked at that fire, and round it they kept warm: where the fire burned, there was the household's focus. The hearthstone was the first block laid when a house was built; it was the establishment's link with the earth, the past, and the dead (we often honour our dead with photographs on the mantelpiece), while the chimney above it was an opening to heaven.

Christianity everywhere uses fire symbolism to express the idea of love, and of light born in darkness, but people who live in cold countries are especially grateful for a fire during the darkest and coldest time of the year; and in those countries Christmas is celebrated with a special energy. The family meets at a place that symbolizes for them "hearth and home." So we hang our fireplaces about with garlands, as ancient Romans once decorated their household shrines.

Christmas cards, tangible reminders of absent family and friends, join family photographs, the family clock, and the mirror over the mantelpiece that reflects the present family circle. Children hang up stockings nearby to be filled with presents from Santa, who will enter the house from the sky, via the chimney stack.

The hearth has always tended to be placed not just psychologically but physically in the centre of the house. Nowadays, if we are lucky enough to have a fireplace, we find it pushed to one side of the living room. (Families are only semi-circles these days.) Yet it remains the symbolic centre of the house. A modern fireplace usually has a square opening, but originally, and still importantly for its meaning, the hearth was circular. Round and quintessentially female, it contained fire, a masculine element.

A hearth encompassing a fire stands for the female and male aspects of the family, for the continuity of the family resulting from sexual union, and for sexual union itself. The marriage bed once stood close to the household fire for warmth, and the juxtaposition expressed the similarity in meaning of those two furnishings. When Santa dives down the chimney stack to leave a present in a stocking, we cannot but admire his dramatic consistency.

A fire, like its conventional accompaniment the family clock, is a symbol of continuity. In the ancient classical world, a new colony was founded by lighting a fire at its hearth—every city centre had a public *focus*, a fire kept burning in a special temple in the town square—from a flaming brand brought from the mother state. (St Lawrence, one of Canada's earliest links with France, was killed by being roasted over a fire; his attributes are a martyr's palm and an iron grill. He is a hearth saint if ever there was one.)

Olympic flames and the fire of the Unknown Soldier are other participants in hearth symbolism: continuity with the past (the last time, the previous place), and remembrance of the dead. The yule log that once burned in the hearth to mark the duration of the twelve days of Christmas was always lit with a brand saved from last year's log. This kindling branch had been kept during the intervening months under the marriage bed, which, like the fireplace, was the household's focus and centre.

The goddess of the hearth in ancient Greece was Hestia, whom the Romans called Vesta. She was a silent, decorous figure, modestly dressed and highly domestic: she never left the house. She was also impregnably virginal. The central hearth of ancient Rome was housed in a circular temple and tended by vestal virgins, whose punishment, if they should ever let the fire go out or know a man, was to be buried alive. The vestals stood for the permanence of the Roman state and the inviolability of Rome's borders: if the fire died, or if any one of the vestals faltered sexually, Rome was no longer safe.

It is odd, at first sight, that the hearth, which is a symbol of sexual union, should be linked so strongly with the virgin Hestia. The reason, essentially, is that there is nothing like a virgin for the expression of steadfast continuity. A virgin daughter does not leave her home in the wake of a man, an outsider to the family.

Every married woman has once quitted her family. It is entirely necessary to the human race that she should do so, and start a family of her own. She left home and usually came to live at the hearth either of her husband or of his family. Part of the ancient Greek marriage ceremony involved the bridegroom lifting the bride (she feigning unwillingness) over the threshold of his house, and her touching the hearthstone and claiming it as henceforth her own; she swore never to leave it and take off on further adventures. Virgin daughters never abandoned the hearth in the first place. A virgin daughter kept her loyalty to her father and his house intact.

Everything, indeed, was done to prevent a married woman from ever leaving home again. But leave she once had. No, none but a virgin goddess was faithful enough and immovable enough to govern the family's altar to permanence, stability, integrity, centrality, continuity, and cosmic connectedness.

Bibliography

Louis Deroy, "Le culte du foyer dans la Grèce mycénienne," *Revue de l'histoire des religions* 137 (1950) 26–43.

Marcel Detienne, "La cité en son autonomie: autour d'Hestia," *Quaderni di Storia* 11 (1985) 59–78.

Louis Gernet, "Sur le symbolisme politique en Grèce ancienne: le foyer commun," *Cahiers internationaux de sociologie* 11 (1951) 21–43.

William Sansom, *A Book of Christmas*. New York: McGraw–Hill, 1968.

Jean–Pierre Vernant, "Hestia–Hermès: Sur l'expression religieuse de l'espace et du mouvement chez les Grecs," *Mythe et pensée chez les Grecs*. Vol. I. Paris: Maspéro, 1974, pp. 124–70.

Margaret Visser, "Medea: Daughter, Sister, Wife and Mother: Natal Family versus Conjugal Family in Greek and Roman Myths about Women," in Martin Cropp, Elaine Fantham, and S.E. Scully, eds., *Greek Tragedy and Its Legacy: Essays Presented to D.J. Conacher*. University of Calgary Press, 1986, pp. 149–65.

GREAT
EXPECTORATIONS

*O*ne of our cultural peculiarities is that we are expected almost never to spit. Most of us, in fact, never even *think* of spitting: it is a marvellous instance of socially induced inhibition, operating in us unconsciously, and at full strength. As late as 150 years ago spitting was thought to be entirely necessary to bodily health: it was extremely unwise to refrain from doing it. "Spit," said a nineteenth-century American book of etiquette, "is an excrement of the body, and should be disposed of as privately and carefully as any other."

If one felt the urge to spit, then, one spat. The question was not whether or even when one did it, but where. It was rude while at dinner, in seventeenth-century Holland for example, to spit on the table, or at the wall opposite one's seat. Polite people spat discreetly, on the floor beside them. They might even, with one foot, rub any conspicuous traces away. One turned aside if obliged to spit while standing conversing in public. But it was advisable not to spit too enthusiastically or too far: it drew attention to the action, and made it hard to find and tread on the result.

In the ancient world, spitting was an aversion signal that people used, rather as a cat employs a hiss, to protect themselves and to discourage intrusion. Ancient Roman women would spit down the fronts of their dresses to avert the evil eye, symbolically to guard their purity, and to show disapproval generally. Men normally spat on the ground before them, to warn other people to keep their distance. Spitting directly at someone was reserved for expressions of extreme hatred and contempt.

Ours was not the first society to impose upon itself abstinence from habitual spitting: polite ancient Persians refrained totally, and Greek contemporaries thought this an impressive, if "ethnic," display of self-control—as remarkable as the Persian insistence on always telling the truth. Giovanni della Casa in his *Galateo* (1558) alludes to these finical Persians and asks, "Why, therefore, should not we too be able to refrain from it for a short time?"— that is, refrain from spitting as long as it takes to eat a meal. Erasmus had complained about people who spat "at every third word—not from necessity but from habit."

Spitting is always regulated in some degree, and spittle

is unlikely ever to have been thought a particularly enjoy-able sight. For more than two thousand years we have been taught to recoil from slimy substances; ours is a culture that is unusually determined to distinguish between liquid and solid. We easily dislike anything that falls between the two categories, especially if the substance is bodily: tears, freely runn*ing*, are fine; spit or snot, which we describe as runny, are not.

Gradually it became preferable to hide one's spitting: to leave the room if the urge came on during dinner, to use the spittoon provided, to cover the contortion of one's mouth with a napkin or a hand, to spit into a handker-chief in the manner of nose-blowing. Next, women—the flag bearers always of new restraints in manners—were thought "never to need" to spit; by the nineteenth century they were too ethereal, too fine to require such masculine incontinence. Once women had shown it could be done, men were also, eventually, pressured into controlling and then suppressing any desire to spit.

By the early twentieth century, spitting had become offi-cially unhealthy; the terrors of tuberculosis certainly con-tributed to society's categorizing spitting as a spreader of disease. This made the practice a mark of extreme disregard for the well-being even of people who were not present when one spat. But it was only *after* spitting had become rude behaviour that fear of germs, the modern version of ancient concepts of pollution and taboo, contributed to an already growing prejudice against expectoration.

Chewing tobacco, with its attendant spitting, went out of style. Notices everywhere ordered pedestrians, restaurant customers, and train passengers not to spit; such signs were common in public places as late as the 1950s. Today, the signs are not posted because there is supposed to be no need; we hope that people rarely even want to spit. If anyone does so, he or she gets a "filthy look" and other signs of disgust and avoidance from everyone near by. Die-hard spitters usually wait at least until they are out of the reach of direct obloquy.

Of course, if you are lordly enough you may get away with breaking the taboo. Baseball players, for example, openly chew tobacco and spit. The crowd look on, contain their disgust, and even transform it into respect for the singularity of physical prowess.

Bibliography

Anon. (R. de Valcourt), *The Illustrated Manners Book: A Manual of Good Behavior and Polite Accomplishments*. New York: Leland, Clay, 1855.

Giovanni della Casa, *Galateo* (1558). Trans. K. Eisenbichler and K.R. Bartlett. Toronto: University of Toronto Press: Centre for Reformation and Renaissance Studies, 1986.

Norbert Elias, *The Civilizing Process*. Vol. I: *The Development of Manners*. Trans. E. Jephcott. New York: Urizen, 1978 (first published 1939), pp. 153–59.

Desiderius Erasmus, *De civilitate morum puerilium libellus*. Froben, Bâle, 1530. Trans. B. McGregor, in *Literary and Educational Writings*, Vol. 25 of J.K. Sowards, ed., *Collected Works of Erasmus*. University of Toronto Press, 1985.

Herodotus, *The Histories* I. 99, 138. Fifth century BC.

Andrew McClary, "Germs Are Everywhere: The Germ Threat as Seen in Magazine Articles, 1890–1920," *Journal of American Culture* 3 (1980) 33–46.

F.W. Nicolson, "The Saliva Superstition in Classical Literature," *Harvard Studies in Classical Philology* 8 (1897) 23–40.

P. Spierenburg, *Elites and Etiquette*. Rotterdam: Erasmus Universiteit, 1981.

Xenophon, *Cyropaedia* I.ii.16. Fourth century BC.

WIGS

*T*he demise of the hat has caused us to pay more and more attention to our hair, which must be consummately cut, daily washed, and blown dry, so that it looks as clean and exhibits as much volume as possible. We think of head hair as aesthetically important and sexually attractive; a lack of hair is interpreted as a sign of age or of ill health. Where hair is felt to be inadequate, therefore, we look round for stopgaps; and even those whom the French call "well garnished" can find ways to improve on nature's gift.

Wigs are already ancient when the history of costume begins. They have often been thought to be harbourers of magical powers and expressive of rank. In Papua New Guinea men annually and secretly make elaborate wigs; their purpose, when the men appear in their creations, is to surprise the women and to effect in them instant sexual desire. Ancient Egyptians shaved their bodies all over, and donned intricate wigs with hierarchical connotations on ceremonial occasions; no one imagined that an ancient Egyptian's head-dress was the wearer's own hair.

Nature has never contended with a culture more incompatible with her than ours is. Yet we greatly dislike any sign of artificiality about our persons. If we wear wigs and hairpieces, they are made, with rare exceptions, to look as though we were wearing no such thing. Fashionable moderns can have other people's hair carefully colour-matched and added to their own by ingenious weaving and gluing techniques. Such locks are called "extensions"; they cost several hundred dollars to install, and last about three months, during which time the wearer may wash them, sleep in them, treat them almost as though they grew from his or her head. No one should be able to guess that they are false hair.

Before the invention of shampoo and the constant availability of hot water, greasy hair was the lot of everybody most of the time, notwithstanding rubbings with a napkin to relieve "swettiness and filth in the head," as Randle Holme put it. One answer, for men, was to shave the head bald, and to wear a wig in public; a cap, at home, preserved the pate from draughts. For about 150 years in Europe, starting in the mid-seventeenth century, men habitually wore wigs. (The word comes from French *perruques*, known in English at first by words like *peruwicks*, then *periwigs*, and later shortened to *wigs*.) A close-cut or shaved head let a wig sit comfortably, and also helped prevent lice.

Wigs at this period began by being intended to look natural: they were brown, black, or blond, and could be made from the owner's cut tresses. The habit of powdering hair and wigs helped cover the joins where toupees and hairpieces melded with natural hair. Later, wigs became almost invariably white, and everyone fashionable was expected to wear one. (Lower-class Englishmen would wear cheap animal-hair wigs, or inherit worn castoffs from their betters.) The young and the possessors of beautiful hair were now obliged to cover their heads; and the richer you were the better your wig. It was an ingenious conspiracy of the elderly, the moneyed, and the ungifted.

In the eighteenth century a good wig was well worth stealing. A wig thieves' conspiracy might include two boys and a dog. One boy jostled a big-wig as he walked in the street, the other seized the wig and tossed it to the dog. The three parted and ran in different directions, meeting up later with the loot. Milord himself, suddenly and appallingly bald, was often less interested in pursuing the thieves than in hiding his head.

Wig-making has always been a labour-intensive craft. Collecting human hair was not too much of a problem: it was cut mostly from the heads of the poor, though even well-off women collected their combings and sold them. Preferences were for white hair, especially that of ex-redheads, and for blond hair because it was easily whitened: hair-hunting expeditions scoured the countrysides, mainly of Germany and northern France, for blonds. There was always the threat of infection, because dead heads during plagues and epidemics provided an obvious harvest.

Hair was degreased, boiled, sorted, and meticulously "turned." (Each hair must be made to point in the right direction, root to tip, because the surface of hair is overlapping scales: mixed directions make wig-hair frizz at once into a hopeless mat.) It was then baked in paste, washed, woven into fringed strips, sewn onto fine netting, cut, and painstakingly styled.

Wigs, pieces, extensions, and toupees are made with almost the same sewing and weaving techniques today. We have invented synthetic imitations of hair, but these are coarse and rough to the touch. No, only human hair will really do. We import it of course, mostly from the Asian poor, by the ton.

Bibliography

Janet Arnold, *Perukes and Periwigs.* London: H.M.S.O., 1970.

Wendy Cooper, *Hair.* New York: Stein and Day, 1971.

J. Stevens Cox, *The Wigmaker's Art in the 18th Century.* (Translation from Diderot's *Encyclopédie*, 1776.) London: The Hairdressers' Registration Council, 1965.

Edwin Creer, *Board-Work: or, the Art of Wig-Making.* London: R. Hovenden, 1887.

Randle Holme, *The Academy of Armory, or, A Storehouse of Armory and Blazon.* Chester, 1688. Fascimile Reprint, Menston: The Scolar Press, 1972, Book III, Chapter iii, p. 128. On the same page, Holme calls wigs *Peruwicks.*

KNITTING

"*D*arkness closed around ... as the women sat, knitting, knitting ... counting dropping heads." Charles Dickens's embodiments of Fate, the *tricoteuses* under the guillotine, constitute one of the culture's few clear legends about knitting. Eighteenth-century women all over Europe, and especially those of the lower classes, knitted wherever they happened to be. They—and many men also—knitted walking, waiting, relaxing, reading, in the dark or with failing eyesight, on horseback, or with infants in their arms. Children learned to knit between the ages of four and seven. Knitting clothed the family members and kept them warm; it earned money; idle hands knew always what they ought to be doing.

Among males who used traditionally to knit were sailors, soldiers, and surgeons (who are accustomed to thread).

Some people claim for the repetitive, measured movements an inducement to meditation. Clerical knitters have included a saint (the Curé d'Ars) and an Archbishop of Canterbury; the recently retired Anglican Bishop of Leicester, Richard Rutt, is a world expert on knitting.

But knitting history is obscure, largely because the craft produced garments so humbly necessary and so useful that they were worn out rather than preserved; it was usually a domestic and female pursuit, and until recently lacking in prestige. The spreading of the skill in sixteenth-century Europe, however, must have been a godsend: knitting solved the horrible problems of form-fitting stockings, socks, and toques. In a world without elastic, and especially in the cold north, underwear at last achieved previously inconceivable warmth and comfort.

The invention of knitting is credited to Islamic Egypt. The earliest examples found have been dated between the seventh and the twelfth centuries AD. Weaving—employing two sets of threads at right angles to each other instead of the single thread worked in parallel rows—is of course far older. The ancient world had known a laborious method of "nalbinding" yarn into a fabric, using a single eyed needle. Egyptians had practised this skill before 641 AD, notably in the production of Coptic socks; but knitting was much easier, quick, and versatile: an entirely new and revolutionary concept.

Knitting was done, at first, in the round, using several needles. Straightforward tubular knitting automatically produces the finish called "stockinet." Canadian Cowichan sweaters, produced by the Coast Salish Indians of Vancouver Island, are worked mostly in the round, and maintain a tradition going back to the original cylindrical construction.

The earliest known purl stitches survive only from the mid-1500s. They made ribbing possible, and also the favoured "stockinet" finish in flat as well as cylindrical pieces. It eventually became common to knit flat structures with two needles only; two or more pieces could be sewn together to make a garment.

Many are the claims made for the efficiency of different, often national, hand-knitting methods. In probably the oldest manner, the right hand holds its needle steady and carries the yarn, while only the left needle moves. Others use the same method with opposite hands. Germans may hold the right needle still as the left hand both moves its needle and throws the yarn. One needle can be stuck into a flat sheath for holding it fast under the arm. In Portugal, Greece, Turkey, Bolivia, and Peru, the left thumb (not the forefinger) throws the wool, which is held in tension by being passed round the knitter's neck, or anchored to a special button or hook on his or her clothing.

On one thing all experts agree: holding the needles as if they were pencils, and poking one of them through the loops instead of slipping the loops onto the needle, slows speed and increases effort considerably. The practice began in England in the early Victorian period as an upper-class affectation, being thought to show off dainty hands. Needles only then became invariably pointed, to aid the conspicuously leisured—and their many imitators. Bishop Rutt insists that in the best technique needles are grasped *under* the palms and held parallel to the floor, even pointing slightly down and away from the body. There should be absolutely no clicking.

In modern times, hand knitting has become manic—and its inventiveness has blossomed—during and after wars; women expressed their love and anxiety through knitting for the troops. The Crimean War named for us balaclavas, cardigans, and raglan sleeves. After the First World War came the emergence and then the triumph of the sweater (which was originally underwear), and the rise of the stockinet swimsuit. With the baby boom following the Second World War we knitted hysterically for our offspring. But only with the advent of mass-produced, machine-made—and now computer-generated—knitwear did hand-knitted garments become high fashion for adults.

Bibliography

Charles Dickens, *A Tale of Two Cities.* London: Chapman and Hall, 1859, Book II, Chapter 16, "Still Knitting." Dickens got his information on the *tricoteuses* from Thomas Carlyle, *The French Revolution: A History.* 2 vols. London: Chapman and Hall, 1857. Carlyle called them "Citoyennes who bring their seam with them, or their knitting-needles; shriek or knit as the case needs; famed *Tricoteuses*, Patriot Knitters" (3.2.5).

Richard Rutt, *A History of Hand Knitting.* London: Batsford, 1987.

Shirley A. Scott, *Canada Knits.* Toronto: McGraw-Hill Ryerson, 1990.

SOUR GRAPES

*N*ow that smoking has been successfully stigmatized as undesirable and antisocial, we have begun to focus on another target. There is growing enthusiasm for getting everybody to eschew alcohol, including beer and wine. The wine industry is in trouble everywhere—not only in North America but world-wide: a recent poll showed that fifty-one per cent of the French no longer let the juice of the grape pass their lips. France has found that modernizing means becoming more like North America.

Not even the U.S. has gone so far as to submit all alcohol to sale from government outlets only, as English Canada has done. But Washington now requires the following label on wine bottles: "Government Warning: (1) According to the Surgeon General, women should not drink alcoholic beverages during pregnancy because of the risk of birth defects; (2) Consumption of alcoholic beverages impairs your ability to drive a car or operate machinery, and may cause health problems. Contains sulfites."

Wine has not always been thought of as unhealthy. U.S. wine merchants have reminded the public that Thomas Jefferson called wine "indispensable for my Health." Even Puritan ministers once referred to alcohol as "the Good Creature of God," and valued its stimulant and relaxant properties. Wine was safer to drink than polluted water, a nourishing complement to simple meals, something to share and enjoy with friends. Even the firmest fundamentalist could not deny the Bible's acceptance of a role for wine.

But the Bible was composed in a Mediterranean land, in the context of a people for whom wine was socially controlled, normal, comforting—even an art form. Modernity was invented largely in America and in northern Europe, the lands of beer and cider and of distilled spirits. In North America, beginning in the nineteenth century, alcohol has played an important social role as a scapegoat: something that can be condemned so that society, having expelled it, will automatically improve, while any need to address other social ills is comfortably alleviated.

North America had more or less to be talked into loving and adopting wine. There was a surprisingly successful movement in this direction between 1970 and 1984, when wine production and consumption more than doubled. But at the same time, Americans were deciding to place physical fitness at the top of all agendas whatsoever—and the lingering distrust for alcohol seized its chance: wine came to be perceived as not only morally reprehensible but also fattening.

A highly undemocratic image, heightened by the mystifications of connoisseurs, has not helped. Wine and its constituent grapes have foreign, often lengthy, names—and hundreds of them. Even if you learn the name of a Gevrey-Chambertin, you still have to know which year to buy—and Gevrey-Chambertin costs a fortune, especially for good years. Purveyors of the Alsacian white Gewürztraminer felt impelled to counter their disadvantage with an advertising campaign based on "Just say '*ga wertz*'!"

A Coke, on the other hand, is a Coke: cold, chemical, sweet, and fizzy. It is pronounceable, always the same, always available, and cheap. (Those who want to feel not only chic but thin can—and increasingly do—opt for plain water, with injected bubbles, in a bottle.) Wine, however, is a product of particular places and conditions, and relies on acquired tastes, complex discrimination, learned preferences. It does not fit the purposes of huge transnational market forces, and modern demands for instantaneous recognition, ruthless standardization, and time-saving efficiency.

One of the most important activities in the lives of modern people is the driving of our cars. But driving makes us helplessly dependent upon other people's competence. A practical measure we can take to protect ourselves and reduce dangerous losses of control is to ensure that drink does not impair our minds or the minds of other people while we are all driving. Working hard on virtuous abstinence from drinking and smoking is personally hygienic and shows civic spirit; it also takes our attention off other damaging habits—such as that of constantly driving.

None of us have time any more to eat leisurely meals, sipping and appreciating wine. We certainly have no time to spend merely communing until alcohol levels reduce sufficiently for us to fall in again with the traffic. And anyway, we love finding something that is prohibited, from which we may sanctimoniously refrain. Especially if we were never quite sure that we liked wine in the first place.

Bibliography

The Journal of Gastronomy. Special Issue: "Wine in American Life." Vol. 6, no. 3, Winter 1990–91.

SWIMSUITS

*T*he insectile shape for women in swimsuits—legs springing from the waist, and abdomen tapering to a point at the crotch—has been one of the few genuinely original "looks" in women's fashion in the past twenty-five years. The grasshopper image, baring hips and buttocks, is partly a harking back to the appearance of the first bikini (1946). The pants of the tiny two-piece were eventually tied on low down on the wearer's hips; but the first bikini-bottom was sensational not only because it was small but because, viewed frontally, it left the body's outline, including most daringly the hips, free of clothing from the toes to the string at navel-level. The one-piece bare-hipped swimsuit began to make its way in 1972, and took ten years to find wide acceptance.

Swimwear—where clothing is worn at all for swimming—has always been closely related to underwear. The same is true today: fashionable briefs uncover the hips just as swimsuits do. The earliest "bathing dress" for women was a long shift, just like that worn under day dresses. It covered the female form from neck to wrists and feet. Women have also worn gloves, shoes, and hats with whale-boned brims as they dipped into the water and battled to avoid the sun.

But a wet shift, as anyone knows who has been on the beaches of countries where women must wear them to protect their modesty, can be far more revealing than even a bikini, and sexier than being seen plain naked. Our ancestors countered this with dresses of canvas and flannel, but complained that these often ballooned out suddenly in the water, with an entirely different effect from that intended.

When bathing, mid-nineteenth-century women wore pantaloons, sometimes down to and tied at the ankle, underneath long skirts. As time went on, European women would leave the skirt off and go about at the waterside brazenly bifurcated. North American women continued firmly to button on skirts over their pantaloons or bloomers—but that was mostly because American men and women quite commonly bathed together, whereas Europeans kept a different bathing time or a different bathing establishment for each sex.

Gradually bloomers and skirts got shorter—but as they did so woollen stockings were drawn up over legs. Bathing shoes covered the intimacies of feet and toes. (Until the late 1930s women displayed bare feet only shyly.) Even when it became conscionable for females to claim a shape that included two separate legs, modesty continued to demand tight armholes and high necklines; buttons on the shoulder helped wearers get into and out of swimsuits.

There was a feeling that wool kept one warm in the water. After sweaters had emerged from being merely underwear, knitting skills created a form-fitting, undraped body stocking for swimming; the human form could be seen at last in utterly uninterrupted silhouette. Men were the first beneficiaries of the stockinet swimsuit. They wore it in one piece, with leggings mid-thigh, and even, at first, a short skirt. A belt was not only stylish but necessary for keeping the suit in place as its wearer rose from the water with heavy wool streaming and sagging downward.

But the stretchy wool suit was soon worn by women too. It, together with the sun-tanning craze that began among the upper classes in the late 1920s, allowed women eventually to display backs, midriffs, and legs naked to the tops of their thighs, provided that a vestigial skirt was retained in front. This "skirt" was removed only in the 1960s—and is said, from time to time, to be about to return, together with the ruched wrinkles still famous because of the memory of Marilyn Monroe.

When elasticized fabrics entered the fray in the late 1930s they soon replaced wool, and men could do without shoulder-straps to help keep their suits on. They bared their torsos and reduced the number of male swimsuit styles to two: the clinging and the baggy, the latter being held up by elastic at the waist. Later, men could wear the tight version reaching to the waist, or variations on the bikini style. Men are said in the trade to buy new swimsuits infuriatingly seldom. Women remain bridled by fashion, which has however to exercise great resourcefulness to ring changes on what is now a very small surface area of cloth.

People still want to cover at least some of themselves in public; most want to cover a bit more rather than any less. This gives the industry some room to manoeuvre—and even, when the time comes, to back away from an image that idealizes outrageous legginess and narrowness, and expresses a generally entomological combination of aggression, energy, and speed.

Bibliography

Phillis Cunnington and Alan Mansfield, *English Costume for Sports and Outdoor Recreations from the Sixteenth to the Nineteenth Centuries.* London: Adam and Charles Black, 1969, Chapter 15.

Anne Hollander, "Swimsuits Illustrated," *American Heritage,* July–August 1990, pp. 58–67.

Claudia B. Kidwell, *Women's Bathing and Swimming Costume in the U.S.* Washington: Smithsonian Institution Press, 1968.

Charles Leerhsen et al., "A Brief History of the Bikini," *Newsweek* 108 (July 17, 1986), p. 50.

Richard Rutt, *A History of Hand Knitting.* London: B.T. Batsford, 1987, pp. 141–43.

Special Issue of *Sports Illustrated,* February 1989.

MENUS

*F*or human beings, a meal is never just something to eat: language tends always to get into the act. A written restaurant menu is a semiotic construct, a food-related literary composition that exists not merely to inform clients of what they may ask for and how much it will cost. It enculturates a meal by drawing attention to the inherent ranking and order of the proceedings, and it also impresses, stimulates, and even intimidates its readers. A menu insinuates far more than it actually says.

In the western world, menus have commonly been provided to the diners at feasts since the early nineteenth century. The custom previously was to lay all the dishes out in front of the guests, tell them what everything was, its age, provenance, and manner of preparation, and then to let people pick what they wanted. Our buffets partly preserve the tradition. Menus, on the other hand, are like theatre programmes, listing courses that will appear from behind the scenes, in plotted sequence. Everybody gets the same food; choice is a matter merely of quantity or of abstention from what is proffered on the platter at one's elbow.

Restaurant menus do offer choices, at prices. Modern commercial menu practice is heavily researched and wickedly sophisticated. It begins with texture: our senses are aroused and readied, apparently, by padded leather covers, glossy embossments, trailing tassels. (Black is "tasteful," orange "opulent," while mere string says "farm.") A precautionary plastic sleeve covering the text gives a robust message, as does deckle-edged rag paper: it all depends on the restaurant's image, which we unconsciously ingest with our fingertips as we ruminate on what to have.

The menu might reflect the restaurant's décor, and be trimmed with a motif repeated on napkins, tablecloths, curtains; it might even reproduce a photograph of an unpolluted landscape, or pictures suggesting the "lifestyles" of the rich and thin. A tall narrow menu, often white and with clean-cut modern artwork, says "cities; slick, up-to-the-minute, and speedy"; a broad format in unbleached—even speckled or recycled—paper with rustic writing means country cooking, regional tradition, maternal meals near warm ancestral stoves.

Some menus are hand-written, perhaps in French Bistro "licked pencil" purple, or chalked on blackboards. These suggest a repertoire spontaneously inspired by the catch of the day, out of simple yet rich stores of honest tradition. Conflicting messages—stability plus change, fun with a solid background—are offered by a heavy durable folder with an apparently ever-new paper list (it must be very clean) slipped inside.

Some food-industry advisers recommend that patrons be allowed to take cheaply produced menus away with them: they are travelling advertisements, almost as obliging as lettered T-shirts (provide those too, if you can). Remember that the lower left quadrant of an opened menu is what seizes the eye first and most securely: put your most popular "anchor items" there, and price them low, because first-time customers most often choose those, and might come back. (Do not put stuffed peppers or strange shellfish concoctions there, for it is a rare clientele that dotes on risk.) More desserts are sold by waiters than by menus: leave the desserts off the menu, and make your staff try them all, then recite their names and properties to guests. Pay waiters a percentage of every dessert sold.

Describe, describe, describe; even print short recipes, especially for complex drinks. Everything must be done to *name*, and then to complete the key ingredients with connotations: many a sale has been clinched by a phrase like "slowly baked to a golden brown" or "bite-sized, plump, sautéed in butter, and served atop steaming linguine." Give imaginative titles to your dishes, if possible incorporating the restaurant's name, to add distinction and aid the memory. "Elite operations" are assured that they may still use French; it sometimes causes questions to be asked, and provides an opportunity for the waiters to deploy their training and talents.

Menus, dealing as they do with food, pluck highly sensitive chords in all of us. For this very reason, menu "typos" and howlers are some of the funniest in the genre, especially when, as a nervous foreigner, one encounters the efforts of restaurants abroad to say everything in English. My collection includes a Venetian *bollito misto* translated as "mixed boils," and a Turkish list that offered, among other treats, "roast dust" and "tart of the house."

Bibliography

Eugen Droste, "Speise(n)folgen und Speise(n)karten im historischen Kontext," in Irmgard Bitsch, Trude Ehlert, Xenja von Ertzdorff, eds., *Essen und Trinken in Mittelalter und Neuzeit*. Sigmaringen: Jan Thorbecke, 1987, pp. 245–59.

Laura Shapiro, *Perfection Salad*. New York: Farrar, Straus and Giroux, 1986.

Margaret Visser, *The Rituals of Dinner*. Toronto: Harper-Collins, 1991, pp. 194–204.

Various lectures and periodicals on restaurant practice.

WEARING BLUE

*P*ersonal preference in dress must always contend with two opposing forces: we want to look different, to express our individuality; but we long at the same time to look like everybody else. Blue jeans, which for the past thirty years have covered in denim the lower halves of larger and larger multitudes of people, are successful partly because they provide a simple answer to the dilemma: they enable us all to look alike from the waist down, while remaining free to be fantastic (if we choose) with our tops. We may rip, paint, and embroider the basic uniform foundation to suit our taste; some of us seek out black jeans, green, khaki, or white; but jeans, more than ninety per cent of the time, are preferred plain blue.

When blue jeans became mass fashion (rather than utilitarian gear for ranchers, cowboys, and farmers) in the early 1960s, they were "protest" clothing: wearing them suggested solidarity with workers, and deliberate rejection of the values of the mannered, moneyed establishment. Both men and women wear jeans, proclaiming that we are all of us vigorous, mobile, and equal—even though male and female shapes continue poignantly to differ. Jeans are populist, liberated, but (in spite of their tough image) obedient—not least in being blue.

When in the early centuries AD the techniques for making the ancient royal purple dye were gradually forgotten, blue fell from grace. ("Purple" and "blue" had often been interchangeable terms: compare the rhyme "Roses are red, violets are blue....") Early medieval blue dyes were what the French expressively call *pisseux*: they faded, and ran; only workers in rough, often-soiled garments wore blue. In Europe, blue has ever since been the customary colour of workers' clothing; overalls, *salopettes*, and "blue collars" survive today alongside American blue jeans.

But in the early thirteenth century, improved methods for deepening and fixing blue from the leaves of woad, a plant related to cabbage, began to enrich the areas of Europe that painstakingly grew, fermented, ground, and packaged woad (also known as *pastel*) in balls for export. The Capetian kings of France took a powerful saturated blue as background to the fleur-de-lis, and the romance of the Western world with blue began again.

Woad was ousted by indigo (from India, as its name recalls) in the sixteenth century, and that trade in turn

was ruined after 1897, when German chemists synthe-
sized indigo. Extracting the dye from plants has since
survived mainly as a folk art in parts of the Far East and
in Africa.

Blue, the colour of sea and sky, is thought of all over the
world as a "cool" colour. It is calm, moderate, and (like the
sky) perceived as "going with" every other colour. Ancient
European sky gods were intensely male. Yet, with its meanings of mysticism, wisdom, and loyalty, blue became the
colour of the Virgin Mary ("Queen of Heaven," "Star of
the Sea"). Blue is now the colour of good women and of
constancy, which is why a bride, both being initiated into
a new life and insisting upon her intention to be faithful,
wears "something old, something new, something borrowed, something blue." When clothing merchants in the
late nineteenth century decided to push "pink for a girl,
blue for a boy," the reason was almost certainly sexist. Pink
is the fleshly colour (though also fresh and innocent)—the
opposite of strong, spiritual, brainy blue.

One of the most distinctively modern ideals in clothing
is that we ought to avoid bright colours. "Smart" people
respond by doggedly and deliberately dressing in grey,
beige, black, and brown—perhaps to go with our concrete,
tarred, and steel city-scapes. Or, so much colour now being
so easily available, we enjoy fastidiously turning it all down
for "classy" discretion. Blue is a compromise: a colour, but
quiet. Never has it been as popular as it is now: a recent
survey established that half of us choose blue as our

favourite colour; and TV cameras endorse our preference by reproducing blue extraordinarily well.

Even synthetic indigo fades—and we would hate it not to. As moderns, we are cool, moderate, and far more obedient than the myths about us pretend; we do not often seek to "put ourselves forward." Virtuous blue is the soul mate of sober black. So as we all keep wearing our casual, serviceable, egalitarian, and unassuming jeans, we love them all the more for fading into a myriad mild but almost cheerful shades of the obligatory blue.

Bibliography

Christian Cau, *Pastel au pays de Cocagne*. Toulouse: Loubatières, 1988.

Keith McLaren, *The Colour Science of Dyes and Pigments*. Bristol: Hilger, 1983, Chapter 1.

Michel Pastoureau, "Et puis vint le bleu," in *Figures et couleurs*. Paris: Léopard d'or, 1986.

Kenneth G. Ponting, *A Dictionary of Dyes and Dyeing*. London: Mills and Boon, 1980. s.v. Woad; Indigo; Blue.

Gösta Sandberg, *Indigo Textiles: Technique and History*. London: A. & C. Black, 1989.

Ehud Spanier, ed., *The Royal Purple and the Biblical Blue, Argaman and Tekhelet: The Study of Chief Rabbi Dr. Isaac Herzog on the Dye Industries in Ancient Israel and Recent Scientific Contributions*. Jerusalem: Keter, 1987.

UNCIVILIZED TO
CONTEMPLATE

A pumpkin is an idea, not a botanical category. Squashes and pumpkins are really the same thing: "pumpkin" refers merely to the object's appearance—its girth, ribbed rotundity, and orangeness. Pumpkins remind people of weird heads—dense, brainless heads—and of pregnant bellies. They are cheerful and unthreatening—which is why we choose them for the masks of the grinning dead at Hallowe'en. Pumpkin-heads beg to be given features; their silliness, and our affection for them, are useful for undercutting the fright.

A pumpkin (from Greek *pepon*) is a thing that ripens in the sun; the -kin is an undeserved diminutive. The pumpkin belongs to the genus Cucurbita, and it is botanically speaking a berry—by far the largest berry, and often the largest fruit, on earth. Squash and pumpkins are New World fruit; before Columbus, only melons, cucumbers, gourds, and their relatives were known in Europe.

But the connotations of the cucurbits were the same as those we give them today: they were useful, sexy (either round and pregnant, or phallus-shaped), coarse, and stupid. A satire by Seneca on the apotheosis of the Emperor Claudius was called Apocolocyntosis, or "The Pumpkinification"; Claudius was imagined turning into a colocynth or bitter-tasting gourd, a sort often prescribed as a laxative. Old World gourds have long been eaten, though without much enthusiasm, while melons and cucumbers are among the oldest cultivated plant foods. But nothing the Europeans knew prepared them for American squash.

They were truly an astonishing sight, creeping and clambering everywhere, among the corn-crops and into the trees. They ranged from apple-sized to huge, and were also round, pear-shaped, striped, blotched, ribbed, lumpy, covered in warts, and coloured everything from green to a startling orange. The girth of the largest and brightest of them was described as "uncivilized to contemplate."

This sort had hard shells, and it was immediately clear that they might be scraped out and used as containers. For example, candles could be stood inside their protecting walls, and holes pierced to let out the light. Soon after pumpkins arrived in France, Cinderella's fairy godmother was given the idea of hollowing one out and turning it into a golden coach. A pumpkin was the poetic choice for the purpose just because it was considered lowly, like the mice who were transformed into footmen.

In America, many of the pompions (as they were called at first) were good to eat; they quickly became bright, jolly, festive fare, patriotic because uniquely American, and associated with the harvest, when they ripened, and with Thanksgiving. Recipes were borrowed from the Indians and adapted to the European concept of the pie. The seeds were eaten roasted. (These were undoubtedly the part of the fruit for which the Indians had originally domesticated squash; later they had developed the amount and edibility of the vegetables' flesh.) Pumpkin "sauce," or purée, and dried pumpkin were prepared by the colonists in the fall and kept in a cold room for winter eating. Thanksgiving pumpkins meant the plenty of nature, gathered in at the end of the farming year.

Hallowe'en is something completely different. Here the death of the year is made to celebrate Death, the human dead, the supernatural on the loose, rampaging among us. Pumpkins are preferably sought, or bought, after a deliberate journey out into "the country." The booty, representative of "nature," is taken back to houses in town, then carved—and thereby encultured. Vegetables are given personalities, at a festival where people dress up as something other than themselves.

Thanksgiving is a decorous, family affair; Hallowe'en is both darkly rebellious and public, the grotesque glowing faces set in windows or on porches to impress and amuse outsiders. Hallowe'en is about thresholds. It celebrates the ending of autumn and the beginning of winter. It also emphasizes the thresholds of our houses, across which bands of costumed children, allowed for once to wander at night, demand and are handed candy; and it is on steps and on thresholds that jack-o'-lanterns are displayed.

We breed special pumpkins for Hallowe'en, and grow them by the million. Having used them briefly for joking with death, we discard them ruthlessly, and wastefully leave them to rot. Yet, orange as the sun and as the turning leaves, pumpkins are good enough to grant us one last glimpse of life and warmth before the grip of darkness takes over.

Bibliography

Diana K. Appelbaum, *Thanksgiving: An American Holiday, an American History.* New York: Facts on File, 1984.

Ervin Beck, "Trickster on the Threshold: An Interpretation of Children's Autumn Traditions," *Folklore* 96 (1985) 24–28.

Ulysses Prentiss Hedrick, *A History of Horticulture in America to 1860.* New York: Oxford University Press, 1950.

Charles Bixler Heiser, "Of Pepos and People," in *Of Plants and People.* Norman: University of Oklahoma Press, 1985, pp. 3–28.

C. Jeffrey, "A Review of the Cucurbitaceae," *Botanical Journal of the Linnean Society* 81 (1980) 233–47.

John Organ, *Gourds.* London: Faber and Faber, 1958.

Jack Santino, "Halloween in America: Contemporary Customs and Performances," *Western Folklore* 42 (1983) 1–20.

Lucius Annaeus Seneca the Younger, *Apocolocyntosis.* (After AD. 54) Ed. P.T. Eden. New York: Cambridge University Press, 1984.

SANTA CLAUS'S SIGNIFICANT OTHER

*B*oth the evergreen and Santa Claus are embodiments of Christmas. He is old, vigorous, and jolly like the festival itself, and also fat and generous—a red, mobile, vocal, male fertility symbol. The tree, like Christmas, is new every year but ever the same. It gleams with fruits and garlands and glows with light during the darkest, most barren season of the year. Like Santa it brings us presents. Not being a person, the tree is a more abstract idea of Christmas than Santa, but it has definitely anthropomorphic aspects; silent, green, and static, the lit tree is female rather than male.

The old German song "*O Tannenbaum*" actually addresses the tree and calls it *du*; in one English version the second

line exclaims, "Your gay green dress delights us!" Like a
woman, it is adorned with hanging drops and necklaces: in a
family, indeed, it is usually the mother's task to dress the
tree. (Father would light the candles; nowadays, he checks,
fixes, drapes, and plugs in the tree's lights.) Its needles and
branches give out a pleasantly unfamiliar scent in the house
for as long as the festival lasts; perfume, in our culture, still
tends to be expected rather of women than of men.

In the sixteenth and seventeenth centuries, the attrac-
tion of the tree was precisely that it had no personality,
and could signify Christmas in an abstract manner. It was a
weapon of the German Protestants in their war against the
Catholic propensity to depict the human form and to use
drama in the process of worshipping God.

The Christmas gift-bringers in Catholic cultures were
(and often still are) the Three Kings, or St Nicholas, who
arrived on horseback to stride among the city crowds; from
the thirteenth century onwards the traditional folk art of
the holiday was the Christmas crib, with its realistic depic-
tions of people and animals in the story of the Nativity.
The Christmas tree was a brilliant Protestant substitute
and riposte: it was nature distinctly enculturated, an object
often man-sized but pyramidal in shape, pretty but indu-
bitably not human, and therefore pure.

Christmas, echoing the general embourgeoisement of
society, moved indoors and become a private, family celebration. In many European countries St Nicholas gradually
evolved into Santa Claus and had, like the tree, to enter

the house in order to do his work. He came "from the sky," like the star placed on top of the tree. The ancient Yule log—nature appropriated, the outside brought indoors for as long as the feasting takes—also contributed to the tree as a ritual emblem.

Catholics eventually took to the Christmas tree, and Protestants accepted Santa Claus; both now occur together, still doubles, in many respects, of each other. The crib is often found at the foot of the tree, under the star of Bethlehem at its tip; the baby Jesus is of course the original Christmas gift. Mundane gifts tended to be placed on a table nearby, as they still are in Germany. When the English adopted the tree in the 1840s, they were still doubtful about cribs, and put the presents under the "skirts" of the tree: if Santa is a phallic gift-bringer, the tree is his female, fertile counterpart.

The star is often replaced, especially in Anglo-Saxon cultures, by an angel or a "fairy." The origin of this is partly the *Christkind*, *Christkindl*, or *Christkindlein*, another German Protestant answer to St Nicholas. This is a female figure—another doublet of the tree—a herald of Christmas, who arrives dressed in white with a red girdle, a bell, and a rod, bringing presents to the children. To keep her decently abstract, her face is covered with a white cloth. The figure may also be considered sexless, in conformity with the neuter gender of its name in German.

The *Christkindl* came to be called Kriss Kringle in America; she merged with the Nativity angels and ended up on top of many a tree. She also became a constituent element in the modern, very American, Santa Claus, who has taken on some female attributes and whose name has sometimes been Kriss Kringle. The lights on the tree come in part from another female embodiment of the Christmas season as festival of light: the Scandinavian St Lucia, impersonated by a beautiful young woman wearing a crown of candles.

Santa is a myth for children, and he leaves presents only for them. These are *found* gifts, never handed over directly; in this they are like the objects carefully hidden in wrappings and laid under the tree, to be taken from there rather than from their givers. But the tree gives to grown-ups as well as children, and, when there are no children for whom adults can stage the coming of Santa Claus, they often continue to entertain his companion, the Christmas tree. Of course, these days both Santa and the tree are increasingly called away from the family hearth, and out into the public domain once more, where their services are required not to give goods but to sell them.

Bibliography

William Muir Auld, *Christmas Traditions*. Detroit: Gale Research, 1968 (originally published 1931).

Kurt Mantel, *Geschichte des Weihnachtsbaumes und ähnlicher weihnachtlicher Formen*. Hanover: Schaper, 1977.

William Sansom, *A Book of Christmas*. New York: McGraw-Hill, 1968.

Ingrid Scherer-Mohr, personal communication.

Alexander Tille, "German Christmas and the Christmas Tree," *Folk-Lore* 3 (1892) 166–82.

Ingeborg Weber-Kellermann, *Das Weihnachtsfest: eine Kultur- und Sozialgeschichte der Weihnachtszeit*. Luzern: Bucher, 1978.

STRIPES

King Charles the Bald, coming upon Count Wilfred the Hairy as he lay wounded in battle, dipped his fingers into the count's blood and drew them over his golden escutcheon. The result, red stripes on yellow, became the arms and the flag of Catalonia. Human fingers readily create a striped pattern. Stripes are regular, arresting to behold, and enculturate whatever surface they imprint.

It is possible for stripes to be exceedingly narrow, with wide pale spaces in between; they then create an impression of tight organization, adroitness, application to detail, and an ability to wait and keep calm, as when they pattern the white shirt of a science professor, an accountant, or a business executive. American baseball players also wear such stripes (the costume is very different, of course), to amaze yet reassure the rest of us that cool skill and calculation is channelling all that raw and massive power.

But broad stripes, especially those of equal widths, are loud; they mark their wearers out. During the Middle Ages they were worn by fools, jugglers, executioners, and prostitutes: people outside the normal run of society. Solid European burghers mostly wore plain colours, or cloth woven with all-over patterns or with borders; so stripes, by contrast, could also look Oriental, African, or otherwise exotic.

The emblematic stripes of heraldry began to be used as henchmen's livery in the mid-twelfth century. Ever since, stripes, even if only on waistcoats, have seemed appropriate for servants, valets, and maîtres d'hotel. And military uniforms continue to be decked with striped emblems.

Until recently the tradition of ignominious stripes was continued in convict dress, to express control over the undesirable and clarity about their uniform classification as such. They also reminded people of prison bars, while making it hard for escapers to hide.

But stripes began to seem chic during the eighteenth century, in wallpapers, furnishings, and even clothes. The American and French Revolutions seized upon the new mode, and stripes consequently became the insignia of modernity. (Americans remain fonder of stripes than are any other industrialized people.) Stripes were bright, popular, attention-getting. Where medieval stripes had mostly been horizontal, modern ones tended to be vertical. Today we consider it a bonus that vertical stripes make people look thinner.

Horizontal stripes persist, but the reference is now often marine. Since the eighteenth century, sailors have loved striped sweaters, mostly knitted by themselves: knitters often find changing colours and so producing stripes irresistible. Perhaps influenced by the sea's waves and horizon, and because of knitting method, they have insisted on horizontal stripes, blue-and-white or red-and-white. The design gave them visibility on the job. In any case, stripes have always suggested mobility and physical prowess. "Speed whiskers," for example, are a series of stripes drawn alongside or onto an object, to indicate its actual or potential rapid movement. The makers of modern sneakers plug skilfully into this tradition.

When the craze for sea bathing grew in Europe during the nineteenth century, the marine motif seemed the obvious pattern to choose for bathing costumes, sunshades, deck-chairs, awnings, and even rock candy. (Tents and sails have always been gaily striped, both as emblematic and because of the need to sew strips of canvas together to create broad surfaces.) The linking of stripes with sport, which had existed among medieval jousters and jugglers, began its vast new growth. The association is still exploited endlessly by designers of sporting fashions.

Bright stripes have now expanded in meaning to include fun, frivolity, and relaxation from work. As a further consequence of the seaside, health, and sporting connection, they are used to suggest hygiene: clean, crisp, safe, and controlled, as in bedsheets, ice-cream tubs, pyjamas (also influenced by striped Indian cottons), and even toothpaste.

Children, like servants, are in a sense "outsiders"—non-adults, beings in need of control and schooling. Nowadays they probably wear more stripes than any other group in our society. Stripes express our feeling, too, that little people should be safely clean, vigorously active, cute, and jolly. Children, like actors and other artists, are *players*, not workers. We, on the other hand, must wait for the intervals of time during which we are allowed to don such frivolities as leisure-time stripes; we dress reticently for work, mostly in grey, black, brown, beige, white, and navy blue; and when we wear stripes at all they tend to be subdued and subduing pinstripes, severe and narrow, in dark and sober colours.

Bibliography

Michel Pastoureau, *L'Etoffe du diable*. Paris: Seuil, 1991.

Cecil Willett and Phillis Cunnington, *The History of Under-clothes* (revised edition with A.D. Mansfield and Valerie Mansfield). Boston: Faber and Faber, 1981.

The legend of Wilfred the Hairy is told in differing versions.

THE EASTER BUNNY

*O*ur reaction to the Easter bunny, his oddities all considered, is surprisingly low-keyed. A rabbit—a *male* rabbit—produces eggs. He turned into a rabbit only recently, and made his presence widely felt in North America as late as the 1930s. But originally he was a hare, and as such his mythology is extremely old.

Rabbits in Europe were confined to Spain after the last ice age, and unknown outside it until Phoenician sailors first explored the Spanish coast in about 1100 BC. The country teemed with long-eared quadrupeds resembling the hyrax already known to them. So they called it Rabbit Land—actually *Shephan* (or Hyrax) Land—*Ishephanim*. The Romans, who were delighted to discover the rabbit in their turn, pronounced the Phoenician word *Hispania*.

Hares differ from rabbits in not taking to domestication,

and in not making burrows. Rabbits, like hares, produce vast numbers of young. They spread, nevertheless, very slowly over Europe, transported mostly by human beings; they reached England, for example, more than two thousand years after the Phoenicians first saw them. Hares, who were in occupation much earlier, therefore attracted the mythology. Energetic, prolific, wakeful (hares were believed to sleep with their eyes open), and sacred to the moon (what we see as "the man in the moon" has often been interpreted as the figure of a hare), they were expressive of the indomitable power of life, forever returning from waning and dying.

The Christian feast of Easter celebrates Christ's rising from the dead; but it is named, according to Bede the historian, after the Angles' dawn goddess Eostre, whose own name echoes that of the East in which she rises. Easter is a spring dawning, after suffering and death, after the long fast of Lent and the dark and cold of winter; its physical signs are light, and fertile renewal.

The day of the week must be Sunday, but the date is chosen with reference to the full moon of the month: the feast deliberately embraces sun and moon, week and month, and is central to the Christian year. In tune with all this, the fertile Easter hare as representative of the moon brings eggs, each bearing a little sun as its yolk, and the frangible shell of each inviting initiation and new life, a breaking out of the tomb.

The modern Easter bunny (bunny means "little tail" or "buttock": a hare's tail was known as a bun) has replaced the wild and now comparatively uncommon hare. He overlays the myths of the hare with correspondences and contrasts with his Christmas counterpart, Santa Claus. Like Santa, the Easter bunny grew from a religious context but now is utterly secular. Indeed both of these emblematic figures leave all religious creeds carefully alone. Christians are pleased that the rabbit and the gnome keep out of their churches, while the secular world likes having something other than religious scenes to depict.

The Easter bunny, like Santa, concentrates on gifts for children. But the rabbit is a silent fellow, without a home or as much as a vague address; he even lacks a name. Santa comes into the house to leave his presents, and gives to each particular child; the rabbit hops about apparently unpredictably, often leaving his eggs to be sought outside, by anyone.

With him the law is "finders keepers": chance, speed, and aptitude decide how much each child ends up getting. At Christmas the dependency of children upon the protecting family is emphasized, but the symbolism of the Easter bunny expresses the opposite requirement, that the young must get ready to issue forth into the world to make their fortunes. What they obtain is a question of quantity mainly, because eggs are eggs, even if made of chocolate: only decoration differentiates them.

Cloned in millions of reproductions as a symbol of life, the Easter rabbit is a very modern, very citified animal. He blurs differences and plays down personal relationships; as a male rodent producing eggs, he even defies distinctions of species and gender. He is cuddly yet full of tricks, irresponsible but offering chance and abundant opportunity; and above all, he has the good manners not to mean too much.

Bibliography

The Venerable Bede, *De temporum ratione liber*, Chapter XV: *de mensibus Anglorum*. (AD. 725) Ed. Charles W. Jones. *Bedae Venerabilis Opera*, Part VI/2, *Corpus Christianorum*, Vol. 123 B. Turnholt: Brepols, 1977.

Charles J. Billson, "The Easter Hare," *Folk-Lore* 3 (1892) 441–66.

Theodore Caplow and Margaret Holmes Williamson, "Decoding Middletown's Easter Bunny: A Study in American Iconography," *Semiotica* 32 (1980) 221–32.

Robert Delort, "La longue marche du lapin," *L'Histoire*, 15 septembre 1979, pp. 82–83.

Edward S. Hyams, "Rabbits," in his *Animals in the Service of Man: 10,000 Years of Domestication*. London: Dent, 1972, pp. 150–54.

Venetia Newall, *An Egg at Easter: A Folklore Study*. London: Routledge and Kegan Paul, 1971.

J. Sheail, *Rabbits and Their History*. Newton Abbot: David and Charles, 1971.

Alan Watts, *Easter: Its Story and Meaning*. New York: H. Schuman, 1950.

Francis Xavier Weiser, *The Easter Book*. New York: Harcourt, 1954.

F.E. Zeuner, *A History of Domesticated Animals*. New York: Harper and Row, 1963, Chapter 19.

"I MEAN, YOU KNOW, LIKE..."

"Shut up!" is rude, even ruder than "Keep quiet!" In the polite version, "*Do you think you would mind* keeping quiet: *this is, after all, a library, and other people are trying to concentrate,*" everything in italics is extra. It is there to soften the demand, giving an impersonal reason for the request, and avoiding the brutally direct by the taking of trouble. Conventional grammar takes little account of such strategies, even though we are all masters of both making and understanding the signs that point to what is going on beneath the surface.

An artificially high-pitched tone universally suggests a disarming tentativeness in the speaker. Canadians are noticeably inclined to turn a statement into a question by means of a rising intonation: this expresses hope that there are no objections, and simultaneously requests a sign from the listener that the statement has been understood. Corresponding politely hesitant questions might be "*OK?*" "*You know?*"

Set phrases ("*I guess,*" "*I suppose,*" "*I wonder*") commonly mitigate the force of our remarks. We condition requests, and add extra "if" clauses: "*Would you* let me have one, *if you don't mind?*" Bad news is considerately hedged: "How far is it?"—"*Well,* it's too far to walk. *I mean, you know,* it's a very long way." Criticisms and advice, too, are politely lengthened and deprecated: "*I think perhaps* you should reconsider"; "*Could you* make this version *more or less* final?" But a reproach is rendered blatant, even as it appears to be toned down, by the addition of "*With all due respect....*"

It sounds superior to give information bluntly: it is advisable to assume common ground by adding "*as you know,*" or, better still, "*as you and I both know.*" One sounds less opinionated saying, "*I kind of think...,*" "*I shouldn't be surprised,*" "*it seems to me,*" or "*don't you agree?*" Canadians particularly are fond of the genteelly archaic addition "*if you will.*" A command, of course, is often sweetened, as in: "*If you will allow me,* or *If we all agree then,* I declare this meeting open."

You can try to take the wind of hostility out of other people's sails by admitting an imposition, or by simply acknowledging that what you are saying should not be said. Brag, for example, beginning "*If I do say so myself....*" Launch into a tirade with "*I must say,*" or "*This is none of my business, but....*"

We sound respectful of the truth while pointing out that we are being vague (thereby pre-empting criticism for our vagueness) in using words like *roughly, basically, so to speak,* and *to some extent.* The jagged edge left by our suddenly changing the subject gives rise to a wide choice of phrases including "*I might mention at this point,*" "*While I think of it,*" and "*Now, I was wondering if....*" ("*Now*" makes a claim for relevance, even if there is none.)

A popular interjection has come to be the multipurpose "like." North Americans like saying "like." The word is increasingly used for "as" or "as if"; and "likely" (which as a child I was taught to use always as an adjective) is commonly adverbial, meaning "probably." *Like,* influenced by similes ("teeth *like* tombstones"), can mean "approximately" ("He got *like* sixty per cent"); but it can also underline an exciting fact ("He scored *like* five goals!"). It prepares us for something picturesque in the sentence, a metaphor perhaps ("She *like* waltzed away with the election"), a very with-it phrase ("That's *like* so not happening!"), or any unusual word or thought ("She's reading *like* Chekhov at age seven!" or "She's reading Chekhov at *like* age seven!").

The particle *like* emphasizes totally new information: "And there he was, *like* stuck in the ice." *Like,* as a hedge, resembles "sort of": "His car is *like* greenish grey." And because it focuses attention, underlines, and hedges, *like* is added in requests, answers, and commands sensitive to others' feelings: "Could I *like* call you tomorrow?"; "You *like* turn left at the corner." *I'm like* can even mean "I think vividly to myself": "He goes, 'Say yes!' And *I'm like*, 'Oh no.'"

Conversational language conveys a lot more than straightforward sense. The rules for such expressiveness inevitably operate, but they are a good deal harder to discover than to obey.

Bibliography

Carl Blyth, Jr., Sigrid Recktenwald, and Jenny Wang, "I'm Like, 'Say What?!': New Quotative in American Oral Narrative," *American Speech* 65 (1990) 215–27.

Penelope Brown and Stephen C. Levinson, *Politeness: Some Universals in Language Usage.* Cambridge University Press, 1987, pp. 145–72.

R. Underhill, "Like Is, Like, Focus," *American Speech* 63 (1988) 234–46.

VINEGAR AND THE
SEARCH FOR SOUR

*W*e taste sour things mostly along the sides of our tongues, which are able to detect one sour part in 130,000. Why we are so quick to notice sourness is unknown. The ability to taste salt and sweetness evolved to induce us to eat substances that nutrition requires; our extreme sensitivity to bitterness (we notice one part in 2,000,000) alerts us to most poisons. Taste, however, does not always detect acids reliably: the acid in citrus fruit, for instance, metabolizes at once, while corn and lentils are actually acid-forming. But sourness does cause us to salivate, and there is no tasting without saliva.

As we grow up we learn to turn somewhat from sweet, and to savour the sharpness in many foods. (Sourness, in all languages, is described as "pointy.") Human societies have throughout history sought out and cultivated sour stuffs. The British, for instance, prized gooseberries, sorrel (the first syllable of which means "sour"), and verjuice (it rhymed with "charges"), the juice of sour grapes reduced to the consistency of honey. Lemon juice replaced verjuice in Europe during the eighteenth century.

Wine left open to warm air was either ruined, or mysteriously changed into a delicious acid condiment that added excitement to sauces, meat, and bland leaves, and could preserve foods by pickling. Cider and malt vinegars complemented the soured milks and sauerkraut of northern climates; but vinegar, most strictly and most nobly, is soured wine, as the name shows: it is from the French, *vin aigre*.

In 1777 the French chemist Lavoisier gave oxygen a name that means in Greek "acid begetter," because he thought that souring was the gas's main function. Oxygen in the air is indeed required in making vinegar as opposed to spoiled wine, but for a reason Lavoisier could not have imagined. After a preliminary fermentation, vinegar is created by a host of single-celled mushrooms, each one-thousandth of a millimetre in diameter, that gather on the surface of the wine, feed on oxygen and on alcohol, and turn the latter into acid. They form a thin raft of bacteria, a floating "fungus skin," or mycoderm.

Sometimes accidents happen—the surface of the souring wine is jolted, or tiny vinegar eels are born in the liquid, rise to the surface for air, and cling, round the edges of the barrel, to the mycoderm veil. The troubled film falls into the vinegar and forms a weird slithery blob, a zoogloea, which will die for want of oxygen.

In the past, vinegar-making methods involved deep reverence for this rubbery mass. It was called a "mother of vinegar" and was transferred carefully to new batches of souring wine to work its magic. Each "mother" had its own greatly valued gustatory properties. It was handed down as a family heirloom, or fiercely guarded by professional *vinaigriers*.

We now know that the real "mother" was not the submerged blob but the film on top of the liquid. The sacred "mothers," lifted out of the vinegar, carried a little made vinegar and bits of the living veil with them, to ferment, grow again, and impart their particular flavours to the next batches of wine. The barrels, soaked in vinegar and bacteria, helped a good deal, as did the quality of the local wine. *Acetobacter*, the vinegar bacterium, travels relentlessly, which is why spilt wine must be mopped up at once in a winery. Vinegar casks are often kept in an entirely separate building from precious aging wines.

Most vinegar is now sold as the background to a myriad bottled salad dressings, mayonnaises, pickles, and sauces. Tomato ketchup accounts for ten per cent of all vinegar made in North America. The process of pickling preserves vegetables, but we eat most of them in summer, when other vegetables are plentiful: we love pickles for their taste, in itself. Vinegar is a mild disinfectant, and used to be extremely useful for wiping over the body to discourage fleas.

Nowadays wine vinegar, and herbed or balsamic vinegar, have become expensive gourmet treats. Most vinegar on supermarket shelves has nothing to do with extraordinary aromas or with wine; it is made very quickly, by pumping and percolating raw white spirit through wood shavings soaked in acetic acid, and diluting the result in water.

Bibliography

R.C. Bolles, ed., *The Hedonics of Taste*. Hillsdale, New Jersey: Lawrence Erlbaum, 1991, p. 172.

D.M. Considine and G.D. Considine, *Foods and Food Production Encyclopedia*. New York: Van Nostrand Reinhold, 1982. s.v. Vinegar; Acid.

Giovanni Fenaroli, *Fenaroli's Handbook of Flavor Ingredients*, Vol. 2. Trans. and ed. Thomas E. Furia and Nicolò Bellanca. Cleveland, Ohio: CRC Press, 1975. s.v. Vinegar.

Theodora Fitzgibbon, *The Food of the Western World*. New York: Quadrangle, 1976. s.v. Vinegar.

Misette Godard, *Le goût de l'aigre*. Paris: Quai Voltaire, 1991.

Le Grand Robert de la langue française. Dictionnaire alphabétique et analogique de la langue française. Paris: Le Robert, 1986. s.v. Oxygène.

Samuel Johnson, *Dictionary of the English Language*. London: Knapton, 1755. s.v. Verjuice.

The Oxford English Dictionary s.v. Oxygen.

Pamela Vandyke Price, *Wine: Lore, Legends and Traditions*. Twickenham, Middlesex: Hamlyn, 1985, p. 38.

MAHOGANY

*T*he dining-room table arrived, in Europe and her colonies, during the last third of the eighteenth century. But it only really took hold, as an object that gathered to itself the symbolism of solidity, prosperity, and continuity in the family, in the course of the nineteenth century. By then it had also found the perfect substance to express all its value: mahogany. In Victorian England, to be asked to dinner was to be "welcomed at someone's mahogany," and in France to keep a mistress "in mahogany" was to set her up in uncommon comfort.

Mahogany had been known in Europe since the sixteenth century, when the Spanish began to import it for use in luxury furnishings and costly staircases. Nobody knows which American Indian language gave us the word mahogany. But it still sounds exotic, with irresistibly rich connotations.

The first European explorers in the Caribbean were offered the wood by the peoples they met, for the repairing of their ships. Their journals praise it in astonished tones for its strength, and its resistance to rot and insect attack. Many ships in the Great Armada (1588) were proudly made of mahogany throughout. The wood's reddish colour—reputedly heightened by the application of urine—was seized upon by craftsmen in marquetry. Its use in veneering rendered it essential to the art of fine cabinet and furniture making throughout the eighteenth and nineteenth centuries.

The use of the wood for dining-room tables, however, had to await the acceptance, first, of dining rooms as indispensable appurtenances of modern luxury. This happened during the early 1700s. The lower classes continued to eat at the sponged-down kitchen table near their cooking fire, the hearth. Dinner had traditionally been served to the rich, in halls or salons or wherever they desired, on boards set on trestles. These were exceedingly simple, and not meant to be seen: they were covered with expensive linen for the meal, then taken apart and stowed away.

The new middle class, complete with rooms for nothing but dining, changed all that. As they became richer, they busied themselves with enhancing the amenities of private life. There was a growing market for furniture that was obviously distinguished, did not take too much time to make, and was beyond the means of the unsuccessful yet not too expensive for the up-and-coming. When it came to tables, they preferred them solid, like themselves and like the tables they had formerly eaten at in the kitchen. Their families and dinner parties were large, and they worked hard at polishing themselves and their manners.

The vast mahogany trees of the Caribbean islands provided seamless table tops up to eight feet wide. Mahogany is one of the most dimensionally stable woods on earth, maintaining, even in great sheets, a magnificently unwarped surface. It carved splendidly—but was so beautiful in itself that it could get away with not being carved at all. It was possible (and convenient) for plain smooth wood to look lovelier than the bumpy excrescences of old-fashioned, overwrought walnut.

Mahogany's prestige was enhanced by its being the product of modern colonialism, enterprise, and technology; it was also romantically tropical. A plain expanse of this dark, polished wood seemed a splendid basis upon which to build the elaborate edifice of an ambitious society dinner party. Tablecloths began to be removed for dessert, and for the British practice of the men drinking port round the table after the ladies had left the dining room: mahogany table tops deserved to be proudly exhibited.

The huge mahogany forests seemed inexhaustible, and enormous amounts of wood were lightly sacrificed to style: voluptuously waving cabinet fronts or gracefully curved chair legs require extravagant amounts of wood. The greed and speed of industrial expansion in the colonies also meant that mahogany was often used to fire the boilers of sugar mills and trains, and for railway sleepers, fence posts, and wooden roads. Younger and younger trees were felled; whole forests were despoiled by lumber-seekers smashing through other forest growth to get at the valuable older and broader wood.

Today *Swietenia mahagoni* from the Caribbean, the original and finest mahogany, has become "statistically insignificant" in world trade. We have now turned to an inferior mahogany, Central and South American *Swietenia macrophylla* (which is often rendered less dense and less beautiful by rapid growth in plantations), and African *khaya*. Many dark woods masquerade under the name "mahogany"; lighter ones are stained a reddish brown to strike the "mahogany" note.

More and more people are enlarging and embellishing their kitchens: we seem to be turning away from the relatively recent concept of the dining room, and relaxing into the ancient practice of eating at an all-purpose table placed near the cook and the heat source. Mahogany, with its connotations of grandeur and respect, does not fit the modern preference for kitchen toughness, casualness, and utility. Scandinavian furniture, meanwhile, has finally managed to render "blond," non-tropical woods desirable to people who are both "with-it" and "of taste."

Bibliography

Daniel Alcouffe, "La naissance de la table à manger au XVIIIe siècle," in *La Table et le partage*. Paris: Documentation française, Rencontres de l'Ecole du Louvre, 1986.

Ben Bacon, "The Impact of Mahogany," *The Connoisseur*, May 1980, 58–60.

A. Gordon and M. Dechéry, "The Marquis de Marigny's Furniture," in the annual review *Furniture History*, 1989.

Henri Havard, *Dictionnaire de l'ameublement et de la décoration*. Paris: Librairies-Imprimeries réunies, n.d. (ca. 1830). s.v. Acajou.

Michael A. Janulewicz, ed., *The International Book of the Forest*. London: M. Beazley, 1981. s.v. Mahogany.

The Oxford English Dictionary. s.v. Mahogany.

Douglas Patterson, *Commercial Timbers of the World*. Aldershot: Gower Technical, 1988. s.v. Mahogany.

Michael Stürmer, *Handwerk und höfische Kultur*. Munich: C.H. Beck, 1982.

Timber Research and Development Association, *Timbers of the World*. High Wycombe: TRADA/Construction Press, 1980. s.v. Mahogany.

Urine to redden mahogany: personal communication, Norma Rowen.

THE JOY OF JELLY

"*P*rocure from the butcher's 2 nice calf's feet;" Isabella Beeton advised in 1861, "scald them, to take off the hair; slit them in two, remove the fat from between the claws." Boil them in water, remove the scum, and continue boiling for six or seven hours. Strain, then leave to get cool, and remove the fat. Boil up again, with the shells and whites of five eggs (in order to coagulate the impurities), skim again, and then place the pot by the fire to keep warm.

Have ready a conical jelly bag, which you have stitched from the very stout flannel used for ironing-blankets. Press the liquid twice through the bag. Add some isinglass, which is pure gelatin rendered from the swim bladder of a fish. Alternatively one might shave bits off the horns of a stag, boil them to make hartshorn jelly, and add that to the liquid. Pour into a jelly-mould, pack with ice, and wait for it to set. Turn it out onto a dish, and serve it forth in the certainty that it will elicit delight and admiration.

Coloured shaped gelatin had been a decorative conceit at medieval feasts, and a sweetened version was part of the "banquetting stuffe" that since the Renaissance in Europe had made up what we would call dessert. John Lydgate, in *The Hors the Ghoos and the Shepe* (late 1430s), celebrated the sheep, "Of whos hede boylled ... Ther cometh a gely and an oynement." Feasters might be presented with shimmering "gelye de fysshe," in which whole cooked fish were imprisoned, as though swimming in their element. The fourteenth-century Merchant of Prato, who presumably did not actually do the work, once decided on pork jelly as a main dish for a party, "to do honour to all these folk without too much trouble."

For the point about moulded foods was that they demonstrated impressive and therefore honour-laden foresight and effort. They showed competence, and control over the products of nature. Jelly in particular gleams in the candlelight. It is tender and quivery (Americans nicknamed it "nervous pudding"), but it firmly holds whatever artificial shape you may impose upon it. There is in addition something eery about its qualities: the French are believed to have called savoury jelly "aspic" because it is cold and slippery like an asp, and often delivered a vinegar "bite."

A further spiral to the tradition was added by the Victorians when they created the seamless, tin-plated, planished and burnished copper jelly mould. Foods moulded into elaborate battlemented forms became an essential aspect of nineteenth-century Anglo-Saxon dining-table display. Blancmanges, creams, and many cakes had all to be moulded. Many a dessert was called "shape," after what must often have been its most salient characteristic.

Powdered gelatin had been manufactured in England since 1845, but was pooh-poohed by purists as offering but little nutrition, and nothing like the texture resulting from honest home-boiled hooves. Paul Wait, an American patent-medicine seller, bought the rights to a gelatin powder in 1897, and created a sweet, brightly coloured product which his wife, Pearl, christened Jell-O. He sold it to a food company. Suddenly, in 1906, all America was buying Jell-O. The word has now achieved lower-case, common-noun status in the language.

Jello was quick (iceboxes by now were common, and refrigerators just around the corner), easy, bright, sweet, and light: consumers solidly supplied with food had begun the modern flight from too much nutrition. You could mould jello in stripes, coat meat and fish in it to keep them fresh for buffets, and suspend anything in it, from fruit to chicken bits or marshmallows. The *Joy of Cooking* calls gelatin "a showcase for leftovers."

By varying the consistency of jello, one may now drink it, or cut it into shapes and eat it as candy "finger food." It is so cheap, so dated (thanks to the jello excesses of the 1940s and 1950s), and so ubiquitous that it has no prestige left. There does remain an urge to touch jello—even to jump right into it, as medieval jesters used to do into vats of custard. Kraft General Foods, the Jell-O company, are often asked how to fill swimming pools with their product for high-spirited parties. They patiently point out that so much gelatin would be hard to set satisfactorily, especially in summer, and that it simply is not wise to risk getting it up one's nose.

Bibliography

Isabella Beeton, *The Book of Household Management*. London: S.O. Beeton, 1861. Facsimile reprint, London: Jonathan Cape, 1968, pp. 708–12.

Bridget Ann Henisch, *Fast and Feast: Food in Medieval Society*. The Pennsylvania State University Press, 1976.

John Lydgate, "The Debate of the Hors the Ghoos and the Shepe" (late 1430s), H.N. MacCracken, ed., *The Minor Poems of John Lydgate*, Part II. Oxford University Press, 1934, pp. 539–66.

David W. Miller, "Technology and the Ideal: Production Quality and Kitchen Reform in Nineteenth-Century America," in Kathryn Grover, ed., *Dining in America, 1850–1900*. Amherst: University of Massachusetts Press, and Rochester, New York: Margaret Woodbury Strong Museum, 1987.

The Oxford English Dictionary. s.v. Aspic; Isingiass; Hartshorn.

Elizabeth Raffald, *The Experienced English Housekeeper*. Facsimile reprint of the 8th edition, 1782, London: E and W Books (distributed by Robert Hale), 1970, p. 210.

Irma S. Rombauer and Marion Rombauer Becker, *Joy of Cooking*. New York: Bobbs-Merrill, 1975 (originally published 1931), pp. 560-61.

The Consumer Centre, Kraft General Foods Canada Inc., Don Mills, Ontario.

SYNAESTHESIA

*V*ladimir Nabokov reports in *Speak, Memory* that as a child he complained to his mother that his alphabet blocks were all the wrong colours for the letters on them. She agreed with him—though some of her colours for the alphabet were different from his. Synaesthesia manifests itself very early, and has been shown to run in families.

Synaesthesia is the mixing of senses so that taste (say) gives rise to geometrical images, hearing is coloured, shapes sing. Metaphors are a synaesthetic device, but they are not, strictly speaking, synaesthesia. For one thing they are voluntary and consciously manipulable. Synaesthetic couplings (A is blue, Tuesday green) are personal, completely automatic, and, in the mind of each synaesthete, impossible to account for but invariable.

"A Black," cried Arthur Rimbaud, "E White, I Red, U Green, O Blue." The first words of his *Sonnet des voyelles* (1871), a brilliant if satanic work, are utterly incorrect. I can forgive them only upon the reflection that French vowels are, after all, different from English ones. In English, A is definitely a clear sky blue, E yellow verging on dull orange, I black, U honey brown, and O black and white.

People who experience synaesthetic couplings are convinced there is an inherent correctness to them, and tend to be surprised that everybody doesn't think as they do. The condition was noted by investigators at least two hundred years ago. It became fashionable to pay attention to it in the late nineteenth century, especially in France, where Baudelaire and Huysmans revelled in it. Partly because it was thought to be too subjective, typical of romantic and hypersensitive minds, and partly because drugs such as absinthe temporarily induce it in people not normally synaesthetic, it eventually became associated with *fin de siècle* degeneracy. Psychologists, who at first enthusiastically investigated synaesthesia, lost interest.

Brain research has reawakened curiosity regarding the phenomenon, which is now said to provide a fascinating glimpse into the subcortical brain. (Human consciousness is like a thin film upon the surface of activities in the brain that lie out of the reach of logic and rationality.) We are not to imagine, as scientists once did, that synaesthesia arises from "an immature nervous system," or that it results from "crossed wires" in the "circuitry" of the brain. It takes

place in the left hemisphere, involves the temporal lobe
and limbic structures, and is thought by some to be evolu-
tionarily backward, because the brain seems to have
evolved towards separating out its apprehensions of reality,
rather than coalescing them.

Synaesthetic people enjoy their mixed-sense experience.
One man ecstatically tastes spearmint as cool glass
columns; another can barely listen to what his friend says
because the friend has a crumbly, yellow voice that is a
delight in itself. People with powerful reactions like these
are rather rare: about one in 300,000 of the population. A
great many more of us have a mild form of synaesthesia
such as my own, which is known as *chromaesthesia* because
it is based on colour. People's names are coloured for me, as
are numbers up to ten, the letters of the alphabet, the
months, and the days of the week. Intensely musical people
see key as coloured. (Synaesthesia shares a few characteristics with the phenomenon of perfect pitch.) Others know
number form, where figures are "seen" as located in space.

Synaesthetes use their associations as mnemonic devices.
They remember telephone numbers, people's names, dates,
and other details through experienced play with synaesthesia; some of them have photographic memories. A typical
ability is that of remembering where on a page a particular
piece of information was read. They are often greatly drawn
to a particular colour, and can obtain extraordinary pleasure from contemplating it. (The perception and classification of colours is a deeply mysterious phenomenon, and

there is some hope that investigation of synaesthesia will deepen our at present scanty understanding of it.)

We hear most often of artists with synaesthesia, because they are most likely to make use of their "sixth sense" in their work; some examples are Scriabin, Rimsky-Korsakov, Messiaen, Kandinsky, and Hockney. All those mentioned are men but, for some reason entirely unexplained, the large majority of synaesthetes are women. Synaesthesia, in its vividness and oddity, is a salutary reminder to us of the wonders of the human brain, and how little we know about it—let alone about the reality it interprets.

Bibliography

Richard E. Cytowic, *Synesthesia*. New York: Springer, 1989.

Vladimir Nabokov, *Speak, Memory: An Autobiography Revisited*. New York: Putnam, 1966. The book was first published in 1951 (New York: Harper), with the title *Conclusive Evidence*. Chapter 2, pp. 15–17. Nabokov's mother was also "optically affected by musical notes." He himself was not.

Arthur Rimbaud, "Voyelles" (1871). Cecil Arthur Hackett, ed., *Oeuvres poétiques: Arthur Rimbaud*. Paris: Imprimerie nationale, 1986, p. 144.

RUNS, WRINKLES, SEAMS, AND SNAGS

*W*hen the obdurately unliberated male gaze focuses its attention on a female leg—choosing one bit of body and ogling that bit is itself an ancient erotic routine—it likes to find the leg smooth, glossy, without blemish, slim yet curvilinear, with its shape preferably outlined. High heels can induce the desired contours, but for surfaces and outlines stockings are essential. Nylon stockings make female legs different from men's. They also render flesh visible but untouchable—at least for the present—thereby dividing and provoking the senses.

It was men who first displayed their legs in stockings. In late-fifteenth-century Europe, a revolution in fashion removed the skirts, tunics, and loincloths that tend to be worn by males in societies seriously committed to clothes. Men strode forth in tight stockings and power-flaunting codpieces. Their legs have never since, in the history of normative Western fashion, retreated into skirts.

Women became two-legged four centuries later. They had worn hosiery all along, of course, a fact that used to be hinted at by the occasional glimpse of a stockinged ankle, often decoratively clocked. After World War I, however, women dared to chop their skirts short, and stockings began their modern rise to unprecedented importance.

For keeping bared female legs warm, smooth, and shiny, nothing was better than silk. And silk stockings were wickedly expensive, setting apart both occasions and people as above the common; they therefore made luxurious gifts. They "ran" too, and had constantly to be replaced: a "ladder" ruined one's entire outfit. Remaining ladder-free compelled women to be careful, delicate, and well financed.

Cotton, wool, or lisle stockings were more sensible, stronger, warmer, and therefore low in status—and far less erotic. Nylon appeared in America on the eve of World War II, so that international availability of nylon stockings had to wait until the end of the 1940s. Nylon was much cheaper than silk, but it was sheerer, and laddered even more readily.

For a long time stockings had seams up the back, which were difficult to keep straight, yet straight they had to be. The line emphasized shape. It rose from a reinforced and patterned back-of-the-ankle and disappeared up the skirt.

A straight one demonstrated control, and constant attention even to the back of one's look. When seamless stockings became the norm in the 1960s, millions who had achieved competence were saddened and reluctant.

Crooked seams were matched in shameful delinquency by wrinkles. These had been a problem for medieval gallants also who, having constantly to salute their peers and betters by bowing and "making a leg" in fashionably ultra-tight hosiery, would annoyingly ruckle, bag, and even rip their stockings at the knees. They are described as moving the leg round "in a circular motion in the manner of a windlass," in a manful effort to save their stockings.

Feet, in addition, meet legs in an unfortunate join that can wrinkle stockings at the ankle, spoiling the important doll-smooth, unblemished effect. Twentieth-century people became more and more fussy on this point, until the invention of stretch thread, which has made any hint of a wrinkle a sad lapse: your stockings are too big or too cheap, or you have worn them more than once without washing them.

In the late 1960s we accepted the miniskirt, a step that would have been impossible without the arrival, just previously, of pantihose. These descendants of acrobatic costume (Monsieur Léotard was a famous trapeze artist) had already become everyday children's wear. The teenage girl's initiation into her First Stockings has therefore mostly disappeared. Suspender-belts went the way of seams. Suspenders, like garters before them, had been hidden, and required undoing before stockings could be peeled off. With their disappearance another erotic prop had gone.

Pantihose, in fact, have enormously reduced the erotic draw of stockings. They are protective, sensible (given the demands of female fashion), and comfortable—or ought to be. If they are not, the discomforts they cause (sliding down till crotch reaches mid-thigh, legs too short, panty waist too high or too low) are definitely the opposite of erotic. They run constantly (and are wasteful too: one run and both stockings are disqualified), but they are cheap. For the time being women remain committed to the dull nuisance of pantihose. We are also learning to be more critical of the Male Gaze than at any time in history.

Bibliography

The Oxford English Dictionary. s.v. Leotards.

Margarita Rivière, *La Historia de la Media.* Barcelona: Hogar del Libro, 1983.

Richard Rutt, *A History of Hand Knitting.* London: Batsford, 1987, pp. 60–61, 67–74.

Joan Wildeblood, *The Polite World: A Guide to the Deportment of the English in Former Times.* Revised ed. London: Davis-Poynter, 1973, pp. 133–34.

CHRISTMAS PUDDING

*F*estival foods with staying power must make us feel that they are old and strange, yet typically ours. They should involve some time and if possible several people in their preparation, and if we can be persuaded to eat them only on the festival day itself, so much the better. For Anglo-Saxons, Christmas pudding fulfils all the conditions.

The pudding is only about two centuries old, but it feels much older. And indeed it is possible to find ancient roots for it—in meat soups and humble medieval wheat gruels. Another component in the story was a great sausage, called "hackin" because of the minced or "hacked" meat enclosed in its skin. French *boudin*, "sausage," is related to the English word "pudding." And real Christmas pudding still must contain the meat-fat, suet.

Only very recently has the Western European culinary tradition habitually separated meat from sweetness. Sugar used to be classed as a spice along with salt; and fruit often accompanied meat. In the seventeenth century, Britain began importing a lot more dried fruit than formerly: prunes from France, currants from Greece (the word derives from "Corinth"), sultanas from Turkey. These were added to meat and grain soups for feasts; the result was a thick "plum porridge." Gradually it became uncommon to include prunes; the word "plum" stuck, however, as a general term for dried fruit.

A momentous invention for British cuisine was the pudding-cloth (late seventeenth century). It did away with guts and paunches as bags to hold food, as they still do only for sausages and haggis. Most family meals were cooked over the hearth fire, in a hanging cauldron. The meat was boiled in liquid, and to it were added vegetables, and balls of pudding wrapped in buttered cloth. Savoury puddings were often eaten as a separate course, after the soup and before the meat. "No broth no ball, no ball no beef," children were admonished: one had to eat soup, then carbohydrate staple, then meat, in that order. Meat was expensive—not to be gobbled down with an unblunted appetite.

"Plum porridge," stiffened, could also be boiled in a pudding-cloth and eaten for dessert. Made richer, denser, and heavy with fruit, it became festive, and in the end exclusively Christmas, fare. Rich people, who could afford the luxury of oven baking, also made cakes at Christmas: the Twelfth Cakes of Epiphany, January 6.

At this feast of the Magi, trinkets such as rings, money, and charms, symbolic of future events, were secreted in the cake, to be found by chance (or fate) in the portions served. A bean in one's cake made one king for the day; the custom was part of the saturnalian aspect of Christmas, where children rule and royalty can be conferred on anyone at random. In the late nineteenth century, Twelfth Cakes began to die out, leaving echoes in the iced Christmas cake—and in the coins buried in Christmas pudding.

The pudding was simpler and cheaper than the cake, and everyone had the equipment needed to cook it. Its shape was spherical until recently, and it was considered patriotically British. No foreigners could make it successfully (many stories tell how they try, but forget for example to wrap it in the pudding-cloth first); nor could they stomach its stodge. There is swaggering, even military symbolism too: Pepys ate "a mess of brave plum-porridge" to open his Christmas dinner in 1662; and Dickens in *A Christmas Carol* describes one "like a speckled cannon-ball, so hard and firm, blazing in half of half-a-quartern of ignited brandy...."

The burning alcohol gives the dark, rich pudding a singular, extravagant yet elemental air; the fire lasts only a short time, as befits festival magic. Traditionally, the pudding took plenty of time to make, however. The ones home-made from old family recipes were prepared between July and October so they could be properly aged for Christmas; they were stirred by every member of the family, from east to west in honour of the journey of the Magi. Our own Christmas puddings are likely to be shop-bought sometime in December, and enclosed in covered basins rather than in pudding cloths. They can be steamed or boiled still; or callously zapped in a microwave by those of us for whom the annual roast-with-trimmings is quite enough to cope with.

Unreasonably solid, fatty, sweet, rotund, calorie-laden, and lathered with brandy butter, the pudding is served once—and only once—a year. It amounts to an outrageous snub to everything thin, new, light, and mobile. An obstinate cannonball from the past, the Christmas pudding intractably sits there, mocking the very idea of modernity.

Bibliography

John Ashton, *A righte Merrie Christmasse!!!* New York: B. Blom, 1968 (originally published nineteenth century, n.d.) pp. 173–77.

Charles Dickens, *A Christmas Carol.* New York: Heinemann, 1967 (A facsimile of the manuscript in the Pierport Morgan Library. Originally published 1843), p. 38. The full quotation is: "Hallo! A great deal of steam! The pudding was out of the copper. A smell like washing-day! That was the cloth. A smell like an eating-house and a pastry cook's next door to each other, with a laundress's next door to that! That was the pudding. In half a minute Mrs. Cratchit entered: flushed, but smiling proudly: with the pudding, like a speckled cannon-ball, so hard and firm, blazing in half of half-a-quartern of ignited brandy, and bedight with Christmas holly stuck into the top!"

Elizabeth Cleghorn Gaskell, *The Works of Mrs. Gaskell.* London: John Murray, 1925. Vol. 2, *Cranford* (originally published 1853). Chapter 4, pp. 39–40.

Bridget Ann Henisch, *Cakes and Characters: An English Christmas Tradition.* London: Prospect Books, 1984, Chapter 5.

Samuel Pepys, *The Diary of Samuel Pepys (1660–69).* Ed. Robert Latham and William Matthews, 11 vols., London: G. Bell and Sons, 1970–83. Vol. 3, p. 293. On Christmas Day, 1662, Mrs. Pepys was feeling sick. "[A]nd there dined," Pepys wrote, "by my wife's bedside with great content, having a mess of brave plum-porridge and a roasted Pullett for dinner; and I sent for a mince-pie abroad, my wife not being well to make any herself yet."

C. Anne Wilson, *Food and Drink in Britain: From the Stone Age to the 19th Century.* London: Constable, 1973.

HEARTS

"I ♥ N Y" was one of the most ingenious advertising campaigns in recent decades. Modern people are commonly disheartened by the inhuman monotony and brutal violence of cities, but here you see the heart, know the acronym, and translate the pictogram; you feel warm and accepting as a consequence. In the same vein—to counteract associations of facelessness and ruthlessness—the world's largest bank, the Japanese DKB, has chosen an iconic heart for its logo.

Cute, cusped, symmetrical, red heart-shapes signify kindness, joy, the love of "sweethearts." They are classified by iconologists as "symmetrical soft closed" signs, conventional because unmistakable, a part of no official system of symbols, but almost universally understood nonetheless. We print them on valentines and playing cards, tattoo our bodies with them, carve them onto tree-trunks, and impose their shape on candy, breads, cakes, bottles, boxes, watches, jewellery.

Yet for most of us a real human heart—what the sign refers to—is a terrifying, bloody, pumping muscle that throbs and shudders inside us, mercifully out of sight, until the moment when the organ is genetically programmed to break down. It is falsely thought of as the "middle" of us, the opposite of the thinking head, which is unquestionably situated at the top. It is set askew—nothing symmetrical about it—in our chests, and festooned with veins and passages that we must all struggle to keep open and unperforated at any cost, even though we all know that the effort must eventually prove useless.

The heart has always been thought a life-principle because with death its beating stops. Aztecs cut the hearts out of living bodies in order to keep the world ticking, and ancient Egyptians depicted disembodied hearts being weighed by judges in the afterlife. People have always thought of hearts as somehow independent—almost as little beings imprisoned within the body. They pound when we are upset; the ancient Greeks speak of hearts leaping, kicking, swelling, even "jumping out of the chest" in response to panic, rather as we can say we have our hearts "in our mouths" when startled. Ours "rise" with hope and "sink" with disappointment or misgiving. Only when it means well is a heart "in the right place."

Greeks did not love with the heart but with the *nous* or mind; their bone marrow was what reacted to the turmoil of desire. Courage (the word comes from the Latin root *cor*, "heart") was located in the heart, and the rest of the virile complex was experienced there also: pride and rage, purposefulness, and the sense of being honourable and honoured, or the reverse. Emotion was deeply invested in all this energetic, essentially masculine, panoply of virtues and responses.

Very slowly, beginning in late antiquity and with powerful influence from Christianity, the heart's symbolic role in the culture of the West has changed. It still keeps a vocabulary of courage and energy, in words like "hearty" and "heartening." The heart of a captured beast used to be thrown to the hunter's dogs, to encourage them in future: from *coeur* (heart) comes the word *quarry*. The organ remains the innermost "core" (heart) of the personality, the seat of whatever is sincerely felt, meant, and desired. But the main desire, the noblest movement of the heart, we now feel to be love—a notion the ancients would have found ridiculous, even abhorrent.

Our hearts have become the seats of compassion, of deeply felt love, and of emotional warmth. The language of hearts underscores the physicality of the emotions: we speak of hearts as "burning" with love, as being "pierced" and "broken"; people may be "open hearted," and even "wear" their hearts "on their sleeves." Metaphors such as these are made extravagantly literal in the image of the Sacred Heart of Jesus.

In 1628 William Harvey announced what was essentially the beginning of modern medicine: the heart was no more than a machine, a pump for blood. It took another hundred years for doctors to discover and describe the heart attack. Before that, medicine had tended to follow the ancients, who believed, in the words of Pliny the Elder, that the heart was "the one internal organ that disease cannot reach."

With the new and terrifying knowledge that a very large proportion of the population dies of heart failure, modern people worry about their hearts, monitor them, fiercely regulate eating habits to protect them, and exercise with dedication to keep them in working order. But that does not prevent us from using hearts as a multivalent metaphor as well, plugging in as we do so to a very venerable incono-graphical tradition.

Envy or resentment can still "eat our hearts out," for example. The image is one that was graphic in classical Greece, and positively lurid in AD 1372. In *The Book of the Knight of La Tour-Landry*, a group of physicians had opened up the corpse of a mean unloving woman, and "they founde a foule orible tode within her body, that grapped her herte with her pawes, wherof they were hougely amer-vailed."

Bibliography

Aeschylus, *Agamemnon*. 975–77, 1025–33. Fifth century BC.

N. Boyadjian, *Le Coeur: Son histoire, son symbolisme, son iconographie et ses maladies*. Antwerp: Esco, 1980.

Louis Charbonneau-Lassay, *Etudes de symbolique Chrétienne*. Vol. I. *Coeur de Jésus*. Paris: Gutenberg Reprints, 1981 (originally published 1922–1926).

William Harvey, *Exercitatio anatomica de motu cordis et sanguinis in animalibus*. English translation and annotations by Chauncey D. Leake. Springfield, Ill.: C.C. Thomas, 1941 (originally published 1628).

Homer, *Iliad*. X. 94–95; XIII. 282. Eighth century BC.

Carl G. Liungman, *Dictionary of Symbols*. Santa Barbara, Cal.: ABC-CLIO, 1991.

Richard Broxton Onians, *The Origins of European Thought about the Body, the Mind, the Soul, the World, Time, and Fate*. Cambridge University Press, 1951.

Plato, *Timaeus*. 70 b–d. Fourth century BC.

Plato, *Symposium*. 215 e.

Pliny the Elder, *Natural History*. First century AD. Vol. XI, section 182.

Thomas Wright, ed., *The Book of the Knight of La Tour-Landry, Compiled for the Instruction of his Daughters* (1371–72, trans. into English, 1484). London: Early English Text Society No. 21, N. Trübner, 1868, p. 139.

FASTING

*F*asting—doing without all food for a limited period of time—should be distinguished from abstinence or dieting on the one hand, and starving on the other. Abstinence is limiting one's fasting, for various reasons, to the refusal to eat one or more kinds of food. Dieting is abstinence, or limiting the amounts of food eaten, for the sake of health alone. "Starve" is from the same root as German *sterben*, "die," whereas fasting is "standing firm," German *fest* (compare "steadfast").

Fasting requires strength, and is undertaken in order to gain strength. For thousands of years it has also been considered a health-restorer: the first thing one did when feeling ill was temporarily to stop eating. Today performing a fast has become so rare as to be judged bizarre and irritating behaviour.

The bodies of both animals and people are biologically gifted not only with the ability to do without food for a while if there should be none available, but also with a complex mechanism that makes a body deprived of food more alert and in need of less sleep, and—some way into the fast—makes the mind much more energetic than usual: this is nature's way of enabling us to find the food we lack. The physiological details of the phenomenon are still far from clear, but they include the release of ketones in the body, and other metabolic alterations that increase protein retention, recapture amino acids, and reduce all secretions.

The difficult part of a fast is during the first three to four days, while the body adjusts to its foodless state. After that, hunger ceases. It does not return for between three and six weeks; forty days, for a practised faster, is a typical not-hungry time. After that, hunger returns, and if it is not satisfied the system begins to suffer, and the person eventually starves. When the Bible says Jesus fasted for forty days "and at the end of it he was famished," it is referring to this *return* of hunger; it does not mean he got hungrier and hungrier.

People have taken spiritual advantage of this powerful bodily resource in many ways: to dramatize important turning points in life (you withdraw into solitude, think hard for a while, pray, and prepare to change your ways); to protest, showing intense disapproval and grief (not eating also makes other people uneasy without resort to violence); to assert control over what are perceived as bodily excesses (as in dieting, but without dieting's endless, hopeless distress).

Religions also use fasting to highlight great feasts by means of ascetic preparations (as in Lenten abstinence), to achieve visions (American Indian adepts are famous for this), and to promote togetherness. There is nothing like fasting together to make people feel at one—unless it is eating together after a fast. (Islamic Ramadan is a striking example.)

Some people cannot fast for medical reasons. In modern mass society, therefore, nobody is advised to do it. This is one of countless examples of the way we now reject anything that cannot be enjoyed by all. Dieting, on the other hand, constantly reawakens and provokes our longings to eat, as fasting does not. Dieting can be torture, yet we encourage it.

There are other reasons why we reject fasting. A fasting body throws off previously accumulated toxins, and in doing so it stinks. There is bad breath, fetid sweat, even blackened urine. (Fasters deliberately retire from the world, but their physical state reinforces their desire to keep other people at a distance.) Now anyone who emits a foul odour is not only shut implacably out of modern social intercourse; he or she is also considered contemptible. We are far more accommodating towards known criminals than we are to anyone smelly.

Another objection to fasting is that modern jobs do not easily permit perfectly healthy people to take several weeks off, without anyone being able to predict when the break will end. In addition, a fasting body forgoes sexual desire as it marshals its powers of survival, and we are conditioned to feel deep shame if we are not achieving plenty of sex. (In the past, contriving from time to time to stop lusting was considered a triumph.) And it is hard to make money out of fasting, although a few imaginative establishments provide fasters (for a price) with doctors in case of need, and shelter—but no food.

Eating, however, symbolizes the satisfaction of a myriad hungers, so that fasting is still the ultimate non-consuming activity. As such it is profoundly unmodern. To people who righteously down three meals a day in the socially approved manner, one who voluntarily gives up eating is a singularity rather than an upright citizen: an affront, a troubling, antisocial, anachronistic show-off.

Bibliography

R. Arbesmann, "Fasting and Prophecy in Pagan and Christian Antiquity," *Traditio* 7 (1949) 1–72.

Kathleen Margaret Dugan, *The Vision Quest of the Plains Indians: Its Spiritual Significance*. Studies in American Religion, no. 13. Lewiston: Edwin Mellen Press, 1985.

The Gospel of Luke 4.2. First century AD.

The Gospel of Matthew 4.2. First century AD.

James Hastings, ed., *Encyclopaedia of Religion and Ethics*. 12 vols. New York: Charles Scribner's Sons, 1924. Vol. 5. s.v. Fasting.

Peter R. Kerndt, James L. Naughton, Charles E. Driscoll, and David A. Loxterkamp, "Fasting: The History, Pathophysiology and Complications," *Western Journal of Medicine* 137 (November 1982) 379–99. (Extensive bibliography.)

Ahmad H. Sakr, "Fasting in Islam," *Journal of the American Dietetic Association* 67 (1975) 17–20.

Herbert M. Shelton, *Fasting and Sunbathing*. San Antonio: Dr. Shelton's Health School, 1934, reprinted 1963.

Upton Sinclair, *The Fasting Cure*. New York: Mitchell Kennerley, 1911.

Daniel L. Smith-Christopher, "Hebrew Satyagraha: the Politics of Biblical Fasting in the Post-Exilic Period (Sixth to Second Century B.C.E.)," *Food and Foodways* 5 (1993) 169–92.

E. Westermark, "The Principles of Fasting," *Folklore* 18 (1907) 391–422.

THE NEW ICE AGE

*B*odily expressiveness—and vividly mobile facial features especially—has been despised for several centuries by northern Europeans. The use of too much body language was the behaviour of southerners—those gesticulating, shoulder-shrugging, emotional beings who were self-evidently inferior to the strait-laced, upright men and women of the north, with their controlled, still faces.

To sit in a modern city bus and survey the expressions of fellow passengers is to realize that modernity pressures us all to conform to the wooden-faced model. North Americans in particular grant the high status implicit in being "with-it" to people who look "cool"—and who manage, it seems, actually to *be* cool inside.

This attitude has very old roots. Ancient sages strove for harmony and peace of soul: "no emotion" was the pinnacle of achievement, and a still face its outward sign. Greek tragedy, with calm masks, was lofty; comedy was frolicsome, ebullient—and generally "low." Beauty, wrote Baudelaire, is like an enigmatic sphinx: it never cries, never laughs.

Immobility and gravity have always been aspects of high decorum. Kings and queens, and the upper classes generally, must strive to stay "above" the struggling, intense masses. The most dramatic way to achieve this is by demonstrating what the superbly wooden-faced François Mitterrand's political party calls *la force tranquille*: a demeanour calm because commanding, and utterly sure of itself. The Queen has been taught to take up a sitting position and not budge from it for hours: her subjects expect her not to fidget, and *noblesse oblige*.

An expressionless mien, especially when adorned with the trappings of power, draws to itself all the aims and longings of its audience, who fill in for themselves what they want to read into it. No deliberate, therefore necessarily limited, dramatization could satisfy a wide range of nameless yearnings so perfectly. On the other hand, an inscrutable visage worn by someone known to be a wily schemer not only demonstrates intimidating self-control but is also a formidable protection and disguise.

Another reason for the impassivity of the upper classes was undoubtedly that it distinguished them from the lower classes who have always felt free to express themselves physically, with a vividness rarely seen nowadays. In order to make their attitudes known and score conversational points, or to enhance the telling of a tale, people would "pull faces," scowl and squint, pout, hiss, and roll their eyes. They stared when they felt like it. (In Erasmus's day this was often done intently, with one eye shut; he had to point out that well-bred boys should not follow suit.) They pursed their lips, poked tongues into cheeks, grimaced, bit their fingers, tossed their heads.

Today almost all of that has been suppressed, in all social classes; and immigrants to modern industrialized countries quickly learn to reduce and finally eliminate their expressivity. Apart from smiles, tears, frowns, and intimations of disgust, almost the only facial signs that have survived are the raised eyebrow and the wink—and they are rarely proper any more.

What is passing is permission to play roles. Roles, as the word implies, are dramatic devices, made for public viewing; they express truths, but are not meant to display spontaneous personal emotions. The repertoire of facial signs communicated *messages* rather than feelings; they were conventional, like speech. We no longer view ourselves as dramatic players engaging a community of fellow actors.

Facial expression is now expected to betray intimate, impulsive, personal reactions—and naturally we are unwilling to give those away. We also fight off personal engagement with other people if they are not carefully chosen acquaintances, and hope that they in turn will know enough to accord us polite inattention, especially in public places. We try hard to stay uninvolved, and to look as though we do not really care.

Modern research has shown that the facial expression of an emotion increases the intensity of that emotion. In huge modern cities, people try to avoid intensity of any kind except on rare, carefully sanctioned occasions. Our thoughts ought not to rise into public view, because it is safer that way, and it is also what is expected of us. If we ever let feelings show, we are supposed to feel embarrassed, and we often oblige by experiencing the appropriate shame. Much safer to be cool: never show that an emotion has occurred. Safer still not to let one arise.

Bibliography

Charles Baudelaire, *Les fleurs du mal.* Paris: Garnier, 1961 (originally published 1857). "Spleen et idéal" XVII, "La Beauté," pp. 24–25:

> *Je trône dans l'azur comme un sphinx incompris;*
> *J'unis un coeur de neige à la blancheur des cygnes;*
> *Je hais le mouvement qui déplace les lignes,*
> *Et jamais je ne pleure et jamais je ne ris.*

Desiderius Erasmus, *De civilitate morum puerilium libellus. Froben,* Bâle, 1530. Trans. B. McGregor, in *Literary and Educational Writings,* Vol. 25 of J.K. Sowards, ed., *Collected Works of Erasmus,* Toronto: University of Toronto Press, 1985.

Erving Goffman, *Behavior in Public Places.* New York: Free Press, 1963.

Carroll E. Izard, "Facial Expressions and the Regulation of Emotions," *Journal of Personality and Social Psychology* 58 (1990) 487–98.

Richard Sennett, *The Fall of Public Man.* New York: Knopf, 1977.

Margaret Visser, *The Rituals of Dinner.* Toronto: Harper-Collins, 1991, pp. 326–29.

"La force tranquille" was the election slogan of the French Socialist Party in 1981.

BRIGHT-EYED,
BUSHY-TAILED,
SERVES SIX

*A*ll that's edible is not eaten. Unless human beings are desperate for food, this is for us a universal rule. Being accustomed to having enough to eat grants us the privilege of exerting choice, of being moral about food, of having "taste." We may also, for complex social reasons, suppress our appetite for certain materially excellent foods.

Take for instance the fact that it never crosses our minds any more to eat squirrels. They are tender, tasty, and available—yet we rarely feel like killing them for dinner. Householders tormented by scrabbling, beam-gnawing, cable-shredding squirrels in the attic may call in pest controllers to put them out of their misery—but few would dream of catching their resident pests and feasting on their flesh; many actually beg to have them chased out but not destroyed.

Squirrels, in our own past and in cultures other than our own, have often been categorized as edible; they taste, it is said, rather like rabbits. American recipes for Brunswick Stew call for squirrels braised with corn, lima beans, pimientos, and okra. Hunters in the U.S. shoot millions of squirrels every year for sport, fur, and food; yet most American shoppers would be horrified to find plastic-wrapped squirrel on supermarket shelves.

It's mostly their tails that save them—and their large, dark, almond-shaped eyes. Bushy, graceful squirrel tails are useful to the animals as balances and rudders, as parasols ("squirrel" means "shade tail" in Greek), as umbrellas in the rain, blankets to wrap round themselves in the cold, and parachutes if they slip and fall. We love those beautiful tails. Liquid, mammalian eyes are also irresistible because they remind us of children's eyes; they compensate for what is after all a rat-head, while fluff both splendid and delicate disguises a rat-tail behind.

No matter how tame they look, squirrels remain wild. They are among the few wild creatures that have adapted to city conditions. Sparrows and pigeons lead similarly clever existences, and rely, like squirrels, on human restraints and taboos to preserve them from being consigned to the pot.

Being wild, squirrels carry mites, lice, and ticks, and may suffer from mange, scabies, and worms; being omnivorous, they will happily consume dead meat and beetles as well as the more charming nuts and berries.

When it comes to taboos, squirrels have it both ways. They are both too adorable to eat, and—as wild rodents—too revolting. Furthermore, they may be almost as cute as rabbits, but they do not survive, as rabbits can, in crowded, cramped quarters: they cannot be factory farmed. They are therefore not an economic proposition.

Excluding squirrel from the menu is a modern *city* dwellers' taboo. If there is one thing city folk are clear about, it is that they are not living in the country. And by the same token, they do not hunt wild creatures for food. Squirrels populate the city's edited and expurgated interpretation of the country: the strictly controlled, purposefully recreational, nostalgically green spaces we call parks. Visitors to city parks are there to *play*: they must neither work nor hunt. And since squirrels in a park are part of the artificial setting, they are, like it, sacrosanct. A park squirrel is a sort of quasi-pet, cute but kept at a distance.

It is sometimes suggested that, where squirrels are too many and too destructive—where they live, in other words, in what from our point of view are the wrong places—it might be sensible to consume them and so reduce their number. But declaring a wild animal to be a pest and also wanting us to put it into the "animals normally eaten" category has problems of its own.

Routinely killing squirrels to increase the nation's meat supply would probably be too much work: they require too much space, and they are too small and too lively to reward the effort needed to catch them. Most of us are unaccustomed to squirrel-eating. It is always difficult to induce people to accept strange animal flesh; it is especially difficult when we are fond of the living animal, are not convinced that it is appetizing, and do not actually need it for food. On the other hand, being offered unfamiliar meat to eat just because the creature is a pest hardly amounts to a gastronomical turn-on.

Bibliography

John Gurnell, *The Natural History of Squirrels.* New York: Facts on File, 1987.

Irma S. Rombauer and Marion Rombauer Becker, *Joy of Cooking.* New York: Bobbs-Merrill, 1982 (first published 1931), p. 427.

Calvin W. Schwabe, *Unmentionable Cuisine.* Charlottesville: University Press of Virginia, 1979, pp. 197–99.

TAP-DANCING

*T*ap-dancing turns human feet into musical instru-
ments. In northern European traditions of percus-
sive dance, the rest of the body is held stiff, head and even
arm movements deleted. The dancer becomes a sort of
human drumstick, wooden shoes hammering, as the
watching crowd revels in a display of virtuosity, energy,
and precision, rigorously confined to the feet. Other foot-
pounding traditions, such as Cossack dancing and flamen-
co, did allow generalized gymnastic prowess and the drama
of arms.

But tap is a purely American art form, a vigorous and
original modern hybrid that took final shape only in the
1920s. Whites brought to it metal heels and toes, together
with Irish and English clog-dance ideas. But drumstick bodies had to bend and flex before American tap could emerge.

The loose knees and fluid spine so alien to traditional ballet postures came from African dance.

It took a hundred years for the status quo (European clog dances and jigs) to take in the breath of new African life. Exclusionary rules and racist prejudice fought the fusion all the way: tap had to live through the minstrel shows (where whites mimicked blacks, and usually only whites could perform), through the separation of white from black vaudeville, and through such grotesque strategies as blacks being allowed to dance in white shows provided they performed in pairs (which prevented the possibility of any one black's becoming a star).

But white and black dancers kept eyeing each other, copying each other, sometimes competing against each other in public dance challenges; adjudicators would often sit under the stage to judge sound quality. (Tap-dancing has kept a competitive aspect: "Now watch what *I* can do.") The history of tap also demanded an escape from the tendency (common to nearly all folk traditions) to dance on the spot: travelling movements made possible the intense individualism that the art now expresses.

Tap is in one sense a baroque celebration of walking— especially, in its final flowering, of *city* walking, the rhythmic clatter of soles on busy sidewalks. One of its earliest roots was the cakewalk, where blacks parodied the strut of whites walking, and upper-class dances like the minuet. The winner got a huge decorated cake for a prize. The cakewalk is commemorated in tap by a triumphant, back-ward-slanting stride routine.

Some of the most characteristic components of tap were black innovations. One was syncopation (accentuating not the straight beat but the "backbeat" or "offbeat" of the music), which entered tap from black buck-and-wing dance, and was derived ultimately from the rhythms of African tribal music. Tap became "easy"—and therefore profoundly modern, for modernity demands a casual demeanour—when John W. Bubbles, a black master, stunned and ravished his audiences in the 1920s by apparently sauntering through what they knew to be unbelievably intricate routines.

Tap-dancing became generally spiffy as well as citified (top hats, tails) in the 1920s. Then women seriously arrived, in the 1930s. (Women have had to contend with high heels and still manage to tap: they are, needless to say, at present dismantling that handicap.) Tap-dancers have prided themselves on personal inventiveness, and many of them have created and vividly named new steps and routines, such as Shuffle Off to Buffalo, Falling Off a Log, Tack Annie, riffs, paradiddle, cramp rolls, breaks, waltz clogs, shim-sham, chugs, spanks, and Over the Top.

In spite of tap's triumph in film, with Fred Astaire, Eleanor Powell, Gene Kelly, and Donald O'Connor, the 1950s and 60s saw the art all but die out. Jazz ballet took over the musicals, rock 'n' roll was too noisy, TV too small and too mean with the required sound engineering. People thought "old-time hoofing" dated, eccentric, Folk rather than Art, not middle-class enough. Tap-dancing became mostly a simple way of teaching rhythm to bewildered small girls.

A comeback began in the 1970s, and today tap has a handful of stars, most of them male and black. The mass craze for bodily exercise has helped. And, fortunately for continuity, tap-dancers need not retire early: they can keep going in great form into their sixties, even their seventies, to teach and inspire the young.

Bibliography

Jerry Ames and Jim Siegelman, *The Book of Tap: Recovering America's Long Lost Dance*. New York: David McKay, 1977.

Paul Draper, *On Tap Dancing*. New York: M. Dekker, 1978.

James Haskins, *Mr. Bojangles: The Biography of Bill Robinson*. New York: William Morrow, 1988.

Andrew Marum and Frank Parise, *Follies and Foibles: A View of 20th Century Fads*. New York: Facts on File, 1984. s.v. Cakewalk.

Walter George Raff, *Dictionary of the Dance*. New York: A.S. Barnes, 1964. s.v. Clog Dance; Cakewalk; Buck-and-Wing.

Tim Satchell, *Astaire: The Biography*. London: Hutchinson, 1987.

BROAD BEANS

*N*early all the beans we eat, except for Asian or African varieties, come originally from America— whether they be haricot, lima, kidney, navy, green or "French," "Roman," or "Tuscan." The Old World's bean was the fava or broad bean, which was cultivated before 6000 BC. Until the sixteenth century AD any European reference to beans—for counting, to mean something of little value as in "a hill of beans," as gaming pieces, to cure warts, as well as for eating—invariably means broad beans.

Ripe broad beans are brown (Homer's "dark-skinned" beans), and fed to horses. Bean-fed horses grow sleek and frisky; stable slang is the source of our expression "full of beans." People eat fava bean-seeds green, unpeeled, and even raw if young enough, or with their greyish skins removed when a little older. They taste rather like green peas. Fava bean-seeds are also dried, and later soaked and cooked. The month of May in modern Rome is welcomed with ecstatically downed dishes of fresh baby favas and glasses of cold Frascati.

Mediterranean peoples eat broad beans constantly—favas may well be their oldest cultivated vegetable—yet they have looked askance at them for millennia. For one thing, they cause flatulence; for another they grow eerily fast; and when you peel one the bare green bean looks like a human embryo, with tiny but distinct male sexual organs.

The great sage and mathematician Pythagoras demanded strict vegetarianism from his ascetic followers; and in addition they were to follow his famous command, "*Abstain from beans!*" Since they were like little human beings, rejecting beans as food underwrote the vast taboo against cannibalism. Eating them was like eating "the heads of your parents." (The idea that beans are "heads" survives in modern English slang: to "bean" someone is to hit them on the head; one used to hear people addressing each other as "old bean"; the word "beanie" means a little hat.)

The ancients believed that soul (*psyche, anima*) was breath, life breathed into us at creation. Flatulence, therefore, was angry dead souls (ingested in fava beans) fighting for an exit. People might also have imagined some of their own souls as well being farted inadvertently away. Words for beans (*kuamoi* in Greek, *iwryt* in Egyptian) echoed verbs meaning "conceive": flatulence was a swift and sinister pregnancy.

Beans were also known to cause strange malevolent dreams. Ancient Greeks, and especially the Pythagoreans, were deeply interested in dream analysis, and among the consequences of eating fava beans was a warping of the truth that dreams were trying to announce to the dreamer, or even dreams that were downright false. Eating beans resulted in perturbation and pollution—what sages and sensible people strive to avoid.

Democracy, in Athens, involved choosing magistrates *by lot*: chance was enlisted as a means of eliminating graft. Drawn lots were fateful decisions, with a "will" of their own. Perhaps for this reason, beans were used to draw lots; when voting "yes" or "no," in contrast, Athenians used black or white pebbles. Some sources suggest that "abstaining from beans" might also have meant not offering oneself for public office. (Beans as "lots" survive in the Twelfth Night Cake or *gâteau des rois*, where he who finds a bean in his slice is king for the day.)

All through history, especially in Mediterranean lands where broad beans inspire both love and ambivalence, some people have found that they suffer after eating broad beans: headaches, laboured breathing, fever, back or stomach pain, even, in children, death. The condition was named for the first time in 1894: *favism*, after the beans.

The main facts about favism were not understood till 1957. Some people, almost all of them males, inherit (through their mothers) a metabolic defect in a red blood cell enzyme, known as glucose-6-phosphate dehydrogenase deficiency. They react badly to eating broad beans—even to breathing in their pollen. (Pythagoras, it is remembered, warned his followers not even to walk through a bean-field.) The official discovery of favism adds an explanation that can satisfy the modern mind as to why this particular vegetable in folk wisdom has always been represented as either haunted or ritually taboo.

It is strange that the very people who suffer most from favism (which is almost unknown in many other places) are also the ones who eat the most broad beans. But researchers point out that the beans contain several substances used today in drugs to combat malaria. This protection, the theory goes, for the Mediterranean peoples who were often in danger of contracting malaria, was important enough in the normal population for fava beans to remain a staple crop in spite of their danger for some.

Bibliography

Alfred C. Andrews, "The Bean and Indo-European Totemism," *American Anthropologist* 51 (1949) 274–92.

Walter Burkert, *Lore and Science in Ancient Pythagoreanism.* Trans. Edwin L. Minar, Jr. Cambridge: Harvard University Press, 1972.

W.J. Darby, P. Ghalioungiu, and L. Grivetti, *Food: The Gift of Osiris.* New York: Academic Press, 1977. Vol. I, p. 89.

A. Delatte, "*Faba Pythagorae cognata*," *Serta Leodiensia: Mélanges de Philologie classique publiés à l'occasion de l'indépendence de la Belgique.* Liège. Vol. 45 (1930) 33–57.

Mirko D. Grmek, "La légende et la réalité de la nocivité des fèves," *History and Philosophy of the Life Sciences* 2 (1980) 61–121.

Homer, *Iliad.* XIII.589. Eighth century BC.

Elinor Lieber, "The Pythagorean Community as a Sheltered Environment for the Handicapped," in H. Karpus, ed., *International Symposium on Society, Medicine and Law.* Jerusalem, March 1972. Amsterdam: Elsevier, 1973.

J. Mager, A. Razin, and A. Hershko, "Favism," in E.I. Liener, ed., *Toxic Constituents of Plant Foodstuffs.* New York: Academic Press, 1969, 293–318.

CHEWING GUM

*A*compulsive, rhythmic fidgeting and fiddling is a common human characteristic that all societies seek either to discourage or to channel into habits they have agreed grudgingly to countenance. Foot-tapping, nail-chewing, chin-fingering, nose-picking, ear-pulling, and thumb-sucking have all received formal Freudian explanations, as have behaviours involving commonly encountered objects: pencil-biting, or chewing the end of your tie. But in the most successfully sanctioned examples, we are allowed to find, or nowadays buy, a special object to fiddle with. Middle Easterners construct worry-beads, for worrying at in order to calm their worrying. North Americans prefer chewing gum.

There is nothing new about the drive to chew, yet not swallow, something held for a considerable period in the mouth. Mediterranean men flaunt the macho toothpick. Other people have gnawed various woods or barks to a fur, or mumbled lumps of tar, resin, whale-blubber, or gristle. The Aztecs had the most pliant and rubbery chew of all: balls of latex from the sapodilla tree, which they called *tsictle*, "chicle." They chewed it between dishes at meals (it removed some of the debris from their teeth), and to reduce thirst because it promoted saliva flow. A Mexican general introduced chicle to Thomas Adams of New York in 1869, and a vast modern industry was born.

Chicle trees will not grow in plantations, so the Indians of the Yucatán and Guatemala began to earn a living of sorts by tapping forest trees for the American market— fighting insects, wild animals, the dangers of falling or getting lost, hurricanes, and horrible mutilating ulcers to do so. Today there are few *chicleros* left; North Americans have moved to plastic synthetics for their gum base. Up to thirty chemicals are required to make gum base, and to it are added sugar (sixty per cent of most chewing-gum is sugar), complex softeners, corn syrup (the secret of combining sugar with latex), and artificial flavours.

There are candy-covered gums and gumballs, low-sugar "dental" gums, and the explosively climactic bubble gum. Bubble gum, the original trade-name of which was Blibber Blubber, was invented in 1906, but improved in 1928 so that at last it could be peeled off the face and no longer needed to be scrubbed off, or prohibited altogether.

It was mostly women who first took to chewing gum in North America, because they were expected not to smoke or chew tobacco. Gum is still a useful substitute for people giving up cigarettes. Chewing gum is supplied to soldiers and astronauts liable to nervous stress and homesick for Americana; and tolerated in employees, who have been shown in test after test to type faster and press harder with their pencils if chewing gum. (You should not use it when learning a new skill, however. And sexual manners prohibit the chewing of gum during intercourse, which proves that people do not really believe that it improves concentration.)

Chewing gum gives enough contradictory yet culturally significant messages to make it an arresting symbol of modernity. It satisfies an infantile urge to stretch and flex our mouths: gum is cud-like and primitive, yet it is now impeccably technological. It is also impressively American, and imitated as such all over the world. (It is *gamu* in Japan, and sometimes, vulgarly, *chingongo* in Latin America where it originated.) It is not food—yet we chew it; we chew it—but do not swallow.

The ambiguity with which chewing is regarded in our culture has to do with our considering poorly defined, slimy messes (such as food being masticated) to be repulsive. Chewing gum, however, *does not disintegrate*, and thereby disarms disgust. It is given flavours signifying cleanliness, such as peppermint, and is believed to clean teeth and sweeten breath—all of which ought to make the chewer desirable rather than repellent. Noisy slurping and a moving lower jaw are not, it is true, part of our conception of the proper. But *silent* chewing (with the lips preferably closed) can help, as can careful demonstrations that the jaw may look slack but the wad is being kept under control.

Chewing gum is perhaps most paradoxical and affronting in that chewing is supposed to be a *temporary* phenomenon: necessary, even enjoyable, but limited to its specific purpose of initiating food before consigning it to the alimentary canal. The chewing of gum, however, goes on, and on, and on.

Bibliography

Robert Hendrickson, *The Great American Chewing Gum Book*. New York: Stein and Day, 1980.

Norman B. Schwartz, *Forest Society*. University of Pennsylvania Press, 1990.

Margaret Visser, *The Rituals of Dinner*. Toronto: Harper-Collins, 1991. s.v. Slime; Mouth; Chewing.

I'LL NEVER FORGET
WHATSHISNAME

"*I know* we've met somewhere. I remember your face"—
desperate pause—"but your name escapes me." Age
might be partly to blame, of course: decreasing numbers of
grey cells. We also like to point to greatly expanding numbers of people met, and constantly increasing knowledge
for the brain to keep on file. Whatever the reason, while
many of us claim that we "never forget a face," hardly anyone seems immune from failures to remember people's
names.

People used to be far more adept at remembering than
we are; our recording machinery has atrophied our memories considerably. Yet any ancient Roman of consequence
strolled about with a *nomenclator* at his elbow; this slave's

job was to tell his master the names of the people he met. American Presidents, imitating the Romans, are often supplied with a similar service. It has never been easy to put names to faces.

The face is the primary human means of expression, a person's front to the world, even the seat of personal honour. We learn in infancy to be extremely skilful at noticing and interpreting the tiniest details of other people's faces. But just how it is that we recognize them is unknown. Some scientists have thought that we might have a special faculty in the brain just for fitting facial images to those we have previously encountered and stored away for reference.

Names are far less complicated, and in fact much easier to recall, than faces are. Indeed we rarely do recall a face; rather we *recognize* it on encountering it again. Recognition is always easier than recall: we can usually read a language, for example, before we can speak or write it. A person's name, on the other hand, is not usually in sight when we meet its owner: we have to dredge it up wholly from memory.

We are easily irritated if, after introductions, the first question is "What do you do?" Who cares what we do? It's ourselves—our faces, in the first instance—that count. The question, however, is an attempt to grasp a person's identity. (It is an awkward cultural trait of ours that jobs tend to supply summary identities.) Meaning is essential to memory, and proper names are usually meaningless. They are therefore normally remembered only in third place: faces first, then identities, then—if we get that far—names. Identifying characteristics, however, might actually block retrieval of a name. A professor I know once met an ex-student whose face failed to elicit anything further than "C+."

Busy modern people are often tired, distracted, and full of stress. All this is bad for the memory. We have little relationship—that is, meaningful connection—with many people whose names we are nevertheless expected to remember. And despite the myth that we are non-conformist, differences among people—clothing, facial expression, manner—are decidedly less pronounced than they used to be.

Above all, we have to take in faces and names far too quickly. It has been shown that short-term memory for such a thing as a name turns into long-term memory after eight seconds of application. If we could take eight seconds to contemplate a face and attach it mentally to a name, we would be very likely to remember the connection. (You must not count the seconds, or you would not be concentrating.) But eight seconds of staring, at a slick modern gathering, would seem an eternity; such deliberation might even be construed as improper.

Handbooks provide ploys for those who would remember names and influence people. One such device is vocal repetition: "Pleased to meet you, Margaret. Margaret, I might have met you before. Were you at the Miami Conference, Margaret?" Another is inventing bizarre connections, name to face; for example, Matt Brown's face might be pictured on a brown doormat. Or we could try memorizing the names of important people *in advance* of the function at which they are to be met. We are chillingly advised to seek out only the people who bear those names, and ignore the rest; we will probably never meet them again anyway. (Modern people often expect not to meet others again: it is another reason not to pay attention to them.)

And when you are really anxious to remember names, one author suggests, you can always phone home and leave a list of the important ones (with identifying descriptions) on your own answering-machine.

Bibliography

Helen M. Clarke, "Recall and Recognition for Faces and Names," *Journal of Applied Psychology* 18 (1934) 757–63.

Gillian Cohen, "Why Is It Difficult to Put Names to Faces?" *British Journal of Psychology* 81 (1990) 287–97.

Thomas Crook, *How to Remember Names*. New York: HarperCollins, 1992.

Graham Davies, Hadyn Ellis, and John Shepherd, *Perceiving and Remembering Faces*. London and New York: Academic Press, 1981.

Harold W. Faw, "Memory for Names and Faces: A Fair Comparison," *American Journal of Psychology* 105 (1990) 317–26.

Andrew W. Young, Dennis C. Hay, and Andrew W. Ellis, "The Faces that Launched a Thousand Slips: Everyday Difficulties and Errors in Recognizing People," *British Journal of Psychology* 76 (1985) 495–523.

SEEING RED

S haking a blue rag at a bull enrages the bull—as would shaking a green rag, a yellow rag, or a mauve one. When we wish to infuriate bulls, however, we shake *red* rags, or red-lined matadors' capes, because we think red is the appropriately irritating colour. Bulls themselves are indifferent to colour, and just hate the flapping.

Human beings have endowed the colour red with more connotations than those of any other colour. Indeed, red used to be really the only colour. Before the discovery of the spectrum in the seventeenth century, all other colours tended to be considered variations of either black (brown, blue, green, violet) or white (yellow, beige, cream, and other very pale tints). Our colour range therefore was black—red—white. There were also "reds" like salmon and pink; copper tones, and often gold, also counted as red (hence Red Indian, and "not a red cent").

In several tongues "coloured" means only "red," like *colorado* in Spanish. Many languages use surprisingly few colour terms, but all of them include black and white, and nearly all have red. In English, only three colours become verbs by adding -en: blacken, redden, whiten. Wine and grape language also preserves the three-term range: there are all the different "reds" (rosé is a recent appellation); but "white" wine is actually yellow; and "black" grapes are not really black.

Red is most fundamentally associated with blood and with fire, and each of those mighty preoccupations can be either terrifying or a basic good—so that the ramifications of red, both positive and negative, are extraordinarily complex and resonant. Red is alive, and vibrant. Angry people go red in the face; embarrassment causes us to blush (a word linked with "blaze": red as both blood and fire). Artists know that red looks warm, present, and near; it attracts.

It also marks things out, and has therefore become an internationally agreed signal of danger and of prohibition: stop signs, red pencils, being in debt or "in the red." Red as "blood" is for war and wounds (the Red Cross), violent criminals (caught "red-handed"), and also Christ's redeeming blood. Christian liturgical red means the blood of martyrs, and the fiery Holy Spirit. Fire engines and fire extinguishers say "fire," of course, and "danger," but also "here we are when you need us," and "we are all of us vigorously intent on putting out the flames."

The dynamism of red, together with its warnings of blood and fire, make it the colour of revolutions, angry people on the march—and finally of Communism and the Left generally. Canada's Liberal Party, like Toronto's York University, uses red mostly by default: calm, status-quo blue, the modern West's favourite colour, is bespoken by the opposition. Yet in adopting red for their colour both institutions place themselves, however slightly, left of conservative.

Red is the colour of passion: hearts, sentiment (the red, red rose); and of eroticism, sexual transgression, prostitution. It riots in red-light districts, red underwear, lipstick, and rouge. Red, like ripe fruit, arouses the appetite; gules, the heraldic term for red, is cognate with "gullet."

Red clothes make their wearers stand out in a crowd, and (if we discount "imperial purple," which was made from extravagant numbers of sea snails) for at least three thousand years red was the most fast and successful dye. A great ancient red was kermes, made from the pregnant females of insects that live on a species of oak. Ancient Sanskrit had one word for both "worm" and "insect": both "kermes" and "crimson" came via Arabic from the Sanskrit word that gave us "worm," and so did vermilion, "little worm." In The Book of Exodus, the word for redness in dyed stuffs similarly comes from the Hebrew for "worm." Mexico later gave Europe cochineal (from the Spanish word for "wood louse"), which is made of the dried bodies of insects found on cacti.

Red dresses and shawls, red shirts and cummerbunds were for "best" wear, and for feasts. (*Scarlet* was originally a superb woollen cloth, so expensive that it was often dyed red: the colour took the name of the cloth.) The wearing of a white wedding dress is a relatively recent custom. One of the earliest "white wedding" gowns on record (the bride appeared complete with tulle veil and pearl tiara) dates from the year 1800 in Charleston, South Carolina. But a bride, until well into the nineteenth century, would usually put on her very best dress for her wedding, or wear the robust, celebratory version of her national costume; it was normally brightly coloured, therefore, and often at least partly red.

The festive meaning makes red one of the two Christmas colours, favoured for balloons, paper hats, candies, ribbons, and other decorations—but also there is fire (warmth in the depth of winter), new life (in the "death" of darkness), love (the main Christian message), and even eroticism, for the rubicund Santa Claus is, as we have seen, a fertility figure, and grossly phallic.

Bibliography

Margaret Baker, *Wedding Customs and Folklore*. Newton Abbot: David and Charles, 1977.

The Book of Exodus, 25.4. Mr. Charles Heller pointed this out to me in a personal communication.

Robert James Forbes, "Dyes and Dyeing," in his *Studies in Ancient Technology* (9 vols.), Vol. IV, Leiden: Brill, 1956, pp. 98–108.

John H. Munro, "The Medieval Scarlet and the Economics of Sartorial Splendour," in N.B. Harte and K.G. Ponting, eds., *Cloth and Clothing in Medieval Europe*. London: Heinemann, 1983.

Michel Pastoureau, *Dictionnaire des couleurs de notre temps*. Paris: Bonneton, 1992.

PAYING ATTENTION TO
SNOW

*T*he vocabularies of all the languages we speak differ
in richness, in their insistence on making distinctions, or in their refusal to note them. English, for
instance, is very poor in demonstratives: "this" for something near, and "that" for something far. The Inuit, however, and the Slave Indians of the MacKkenzie River, have
up to thirty different words expressing specific locations,
such as "that in there," "that high up there," and "that—
unseen." The theory is that words accurately pinpointing
places are especially useful to people in hunting cultures.

Arabs use many words both denoting and describing
"horse" and "camel"; Australian languages have lists of
terms for different kinds of hole, and for the variations in

298 The Way We Are

sand. English is peculiarly interested in the forms and functions of motor vehicles: car, lorry, van, bus, streetcar, truck, jeep, taxi, tractor, and so on.

In Hopi, everything that flies—insects, planes, pilots, everything except birds—is denoted by one word, *masa'y-taka*. This does not mean that a Hopi speaker cannot conceive what, say, a helicopter could be. There used to be a theory that if a language has no term for something, a speaker of that language lacks the concept. The idea has been largely discredited. Languages use circumlocutions; translations, and if necessary explanations, are always possible. But it remains true that richness of vocabulary is a pointer to the importance a culture places upon certain regions of the real rather than upon others.

One of the most famous examples of verbal differentiation is the Eskimo panoply of designations for snow. Their number of separate terms for ice is almost as large. The Inuit need words that not only distinguish between different kinds of snow, but also words that refer to the advisability of travel, given weather conditions. The following—a selection merely—gives some idea of the sensory attentiveness and discrimination that is built into the actual components of the language. The list might help to sharpen our own awareness.

There is snowflake, *qannik*; recently fallen snow, *qannitaq*; snow roughened by rain and frost, *kavisilaq*; melting snow, *mannguq*; a fine coat of powdered snow, *minguliq*; crystalline snow, usually found under other snow levels, that breaks down, separates, and looks like rough salt, *pukak*; the very first snowfall of autumn, *apinngaut*.

Snow with a hard crust that gives under one's steps is *katakartanaq* (but whenever snow or ice breaks under the weight of a person standing on it and he or she falls from a height, a special word is called for: *katappuq*). Soft snow on the ground is *maujaq*; snow that is difficult to travel on because it is melting and therefore too soft, *aumannaq*; very hard compressed and frozen snow, *aniugaviniq*; mixed snow and water that is thawing, *aqillupiaq*; snow that has thawed and has refrozen with an iced surface, *qiasuqaq*.

While still in the air, snow requires a different set of terms entirely. Blowing snow is *piqtuluk*; falling wet snow, *masak*, fine snow carried by the wind, *natiruvaaq*; very light snow falling in still air, *qanniapaluk*; and so on.

Once snow has fallen, it becomes important to describe the landscape it has created. Snow on the ground is *aputi*, sparkling snow *pataqun*, a long large snowdrift *qimutjuk*, a small snowdrift or ripple *quyuqlak*, something with snow drifted over it so you can't see what it is *apiyaq*, a thin coat of soft snow deposited on an object *piirturiniq*, a drift of hard snow *sitilluqaaq*, and snow resting on cold water *qanisqinik*. A stick to measure the depth of snow is *havgun*. If something shows up from under snow, you say "*Hatqummiqtuq*."

In Inuktitut, a snowhouse is *illu*. A place where there is the right kind of snow for cutting snowblocks is *auvvivik*, a snowblock *saviujartuaq*, a hole made in the surface of the snow by cutting out a block *saviutsaq*, melting snow used as cement for the snowhouse *sirmiq*. If powdery snow comes into the house through a window or door, you exclaim "*Natiruvittuq*." Frost formed inside a house, in garments, or on glasses is *ilu*, but snow on clothes or boots is *ayak*. Snow collected for melting into water is called *aniu*.

A snowball made by rolling snow on the ground (*atsakaaq*) is quite different from a snowball made by packing it in the hand for throwing (*milluuti*). And I shall be looking out this winter for a snowdrift that happens to be shaped by the wind so that its profile resembles a duck's head. If I find one I shall be able to designate it with Arctic precision, not to say pedantry: *qayuqhak*.

Bibliography

Basic Siglit Inuvialuit Eskimo Dictionary. Inuvik: Committee for Original Peoples Entitlement, 1984.

Basic Uummarmuit Eskimo Dictionary. Inuvik: Committee for Original Peoples Entitlement, 1984.

Keith H. Basso, "Ice and Travel among the Fort Norman Slave: Folk Taxonomies and Cultural Rules," *Language in Society* 1 (1972) 31–49.

David Crystal, *The Cambridge Encyclopedia of Language.* Cambridge University Press, 1987. s.v. Eskimo; Sapir-Whorf Hypothesis.

Louis-Jacques Dorais, "The Canadian Inuit and Their Language," in D.R.F. Collis, ed., *Arctic Languages: An Awakening.* Paris: Unesco, 1990.

Ronald Lowe, *Basic Kangiryuarmuit Eskimo Dictionary.* Inuvik: Committee for Original Peoples Entitlement, 1983.

R.K. Nelson, "Eskimo Sea-Ice Terminology," in *Hunters of the Northern Ice.* University of Chicago Press, 1969, pp. 398–403.

Lucien Schneider, O.M.I., *Ulirnaisigutit.* Trans. from French, D.R.F. Collis. Québec: Les Presses de l'Université Laval, 1985.

SOUP OF THE EVENING,

BEAUTIFUL SOUP

*Z*uppa inglese, "English soup," is a sweet and alcoholic
cake-and-cream trifle. Its name, which has been
dated to the Napoleonic era, is an Italian joke at the
expense of Anglo-Saxon tastes in food. Yet zuppa inglese—
baked farinaceous material soaked in liquid—*is* a kind of soup.

The very first cereals eaten by humankind were grilled,
pounded, then soaked in water, to make them easier to
swallow. In about 9000 BC came the first discovery of pottery; it caused a culinary revolution. Vessels could now be
made in whatever size and shape people liked, and in them
we could heat water and keep it boiling while we cooked
our food in it. Meat and vegetables could then be served
either together with, or separately from, the broth that had

absorbed flavour from them. Broth (the word, like *bouillon*, means "something boiled") could also be poured over our grilled—and now also boiled—cereal mashes, liquid over solid, the way we still serve porridge with milk.

Moistened mash is the basis for beer, and also the beginning of bread. The two great inventions, beer and yeast-raised bread, are interconnected—ancient Egyptian bakeries and breweries were often on the same premises—and many archaeologists believe that beer, a simpler basic preparation with no need of ovens, came first. Bread-baking produced a substance that began to replace the ancient cereal mashes.

Leftover bread (after all the work and expense that goes into producing a loaf) dries out; an obvious way to render it edible again is to wet it—with water, wine, milk, beer, or broth. A piece of bread is a sop or sippet (French *soupe*) that you supped or sipped. (A sentimental person is "soppy" like soaked bread.) Eating broth with a *soupe* in it became for all bread-based cuisines the easiest, most economical means of normal nourishment. It came to constitute a mostly evening meal, called *supper*.

Soupe remains the word in French for a rich, dense, though still liquid preparation; if thick enough it is a meal in itself. A broth with no bread in it, though sometimes with croutons floating on it, and served separately from meats and vegetables that make up the rest of the meal, is called *potage*, from Latin *potare*, to drink.

But soup is so redolent of health, sustenance, and nutrition that it is always thought of as food rather than drink, even when it is only the overture to a banquet; it is therefore *eaten*, though liquid, with a spoon. Wine is not drunk with a first course of soup because soup is liquid already, and because we wish to ensure that everybody present has consumed something before starting on the wine. *Potare*, the reference to liquidity, is also the root of *pottage* (like Esau's mess, probably of red lentils) and *pottery*. The French think so naturally that their vegetable gardens are for making soup that they call them *potagers*.

Cereals, meats, and vegetables in broth, once on the cutting edge of technology because of the mastery of fire they presuppose, now seem an immemorially ancient, archetypal food. Soups can be national treasures, central to a people's identity: think of bouillabaisse, gazpacho, beer soups, onion soup, goulash, gumbo, pot-au-feu, Scotch broth, borscht, minestrone, and pasta in brodo. Soups are eaten hot and cold, and vary infinitely in consistency. Pasta in *brodo* (broth) is transformed into a dish of solids simply by thickening the liquid component into a sauce and serving the pasta under rather than in it.

Soup is homely food, but essential to people's sense of well-being. Mashes and soups were very early on used for military rations: ancient Greek soldiers, for instance, carried with them a sack of prepared barley-meal and some wine; you boiled water (or, if you had to, left it cold), added *madza*, mixed, and *voilà*. Restaurants derive their name from a Paris establishment that offered only soups: it advertised them, in 1765, as *restaurants divins*, "divine restorers."

The desire to carry soup on the person or to have it instantly and easily available finally led to another food revolution, the invention of the first modern "convenience" foods: soup bottled (1809), canned (1812), and dehydrated (mid-nineteenth century). Earlier still (1724) we had "pocket soup" concentrated in tablet form; Casanova wrote that he never left home without it. And in 1864 the cattle herds of Uruguay began to be boiled down into meat extracts and bouillon cubes.

Bibliography

Archilochus 2; in David A. Campbell, ed., *Greek Lyric Poetry*. London: Macmillan, 1967, p. 1.

Jacques Barrau, *Les Hommes et leurs aliments*. Paris: Messidor/Temps Actuels, 1983, Chapter 3.

The Book of Genesis, 25.29–34.

Lewis Carroll, *Alice's Adventures in Wonderland*. In *The Complete Works of Lewis Carroll*. New York: The Modern Library, Random House, 1965, p. 113, the Mock Turtle's Song. (first published 1865.)

Casanova, Jacques (Giacomo) de Seingalt, *Histoire de ma vie*. 12 vols., Vol. 9, Chapter 2. Paris: Plon, 1959, Vol. 5, p. 34. The boat journey during which Casanova ate "pocket soup" took place in 1763.

Léo Moulin, *Les Liturgies de la table*. Paris: Albin Michel, 1988.

Richard Olney, *Simple French Food*. Toronto: McClelland and Stewart, 1974, pp. 210–27.

Fritz Ruf, "Die Suppe in der Geschichte der Ernährung," in Irmgard Bitsch, Trude Ehlert, and Xenja von Ertzdorff, eds., *Essen und Trinken in Mittelalter und Neuzeit*. Sigmaringen: Jan Thorbecke, 1987, pp. 165–81.

Hans-Jürgen Teuteberg, *Die Rolle des Fleischextrakts für die Ernährungswissenschaften und den Aufstieg der Suppenindustrie*. Stuttgart: Franz Steiner, 1990.

INDEX

A

Absinthe, 238
Abstinence, 180, 257, 278; see also Lent;
    Taboos, food
Accountants, 207
Acrobats, 148, 244
Actors, Acting, 210, 264
Adams, Thomas, 283
Adolescents, 105
Advertizing, 4, 24, 179, 188–90, 252, 304–5
Aeschylus, 256
Africans, 68, 88, 194, 208, 230, 273, 274, 277
Age, 3, 4, 8, 9, 62, 64, 74, 152, 167, 169,
    202, 275, 287
Aggressiveness, 39, 63, 65, 95–96, 185
Agriculture, 67–68
Airplanes, 1–5
Alcohol, 177–81, 223, 249
Americans, Central and South, 230, 277,
    284; see also Indians, American; Aztecs;
    also citizens of individual countries.
Americans, North, 2, 3, 11, 12, 13, 18, 22,
    28, 29, 32, 59, 68, 69–70, 77–78, 82–86,
    94, 95, 113, 117–18, 120, 133, 134, 143,
    147–48, 177–78, 183, 192–96, 199–200,
    204–5, 207–8, 212, 219, 224, 233, 234,
    243, 262, 268, 272–76, 282–86, 288,
    295, 297–301
Androgyny, 33, 95–96
Angels, 204–5
Animals, 26–31, 32, 33, 34, 39, 40, 48, 50,
    60, 69, 94, 95, 112, 117–21, 127, 153,
    169, 203, 212–14, 254, 255, 267–71,
    277, 283
Answering-machines, 290
Aphrodisiacs, 70
Arabs, 173, 294, 297
Archilochus, 306
Architects, 122, 123
Armenians, 119–20
Artificiality, opposition to, 168; see also
    Informality.
Artists, 240, 293
Assyrians, ancient, 63
Astaire, Fred, 274
Athenaeus, 121
Audubon, John James, 26, 31
Australian Aborigines, 297–98
Avocados, 67–71
Aztecs, 44, 70, 253, 283

B

Bagels, 42
Baldness, 62, 168, 169, 207
Baptism, 7, 133
Bar Mitzvah, 7

Barley, 304
Baseball, 165, 207–8
Bathing-machines, 16
Bathtubs, 137, 138, 139
Baudelaire, Charles, 238, 263, 266
Beans, 249, 277; Baked, 42–47; Haricot, 44,
    45, 277. see also Fava Beans.
Beards, 27, 32, 62–66
Beauty, 3–4, 9, 169, 263.
Beauty queens, 38
Bede, The Venerable, 213
Beds, 150, 158, 159. Bedclothes, 209
Beer, 8, 177, 178, 303
Beeton, Isabella, 232–33, 236
Bell, Alexander Graham, 108
Bells, 107–11, 204
Bible, 178, 196, 258, 261, 294, 296, 304,
    306
Birds, 26–31, 114, 133–34, 268.
    Eaten at celebrations, 29–30
Bitterness, 222
Black, 188, 194, 195, 210, 292, 293
Blancmanges, 234
Blood symbolism, 207, 293, 294
Blue, 23, 192–96, 209, 210, 294. Blue col-
    lars, 193
Blushing, 47–51, 98, 99, 101, 293
Body markings, 7, 9, 17; see also Tattoos.
Bolivians, 174
Boots, 17, 32, 37, 95
Bouillon cubes, 305
Bowing, 58, 59, 244
Brain, 129–30, 144, 238–40, 258, 287, 288
Brandy, 249, 252. Brandy butter, 250
Brazilians, 68, 87–88
Bread, 303
British, 13, 16, 27, 28, 29, 30, 44, 57, 58, 64,
    78, 79, 82–86, 87–88, 100, 109, 113, 119,
    128, 129, 132–36, 143, 169, 174–75,
    202–3, 204, 213, 223, 227, 229, 233–34,
    247, 272, 297, 298, 302
Broad beans, see also Fava beans.
Brown, 194, 210
Bubbles, John W., 274
Bulgarians, 89
Bulls, 292
Burmese, 91
Business executives, 207

C

Cakes, 43, 234, 248–49, 253, 273–74, 279,
    302; see also Wedding cakes.
Canadians, 28, 29, 42, 77, 117, 134, 159,
    174, 177, 217–18, 294, 297–301
Cancer, 9, 19
Candy, 94, 114, 200, 209, 214, 234, 253,
    295; see also Chewing gum
Canned food, 45, 305
Cannibalism, 278
Caribbean, 68, 69, 228, 229–30; see also Jamaicans

Carlyle, Thomas, 176
Carroll, Lewis, 306
Cars, 90, 93, 94, 107, 178, 179–80, 298.
    Car valets, 72
Casanova, Jacques (Giacomo) de Seingalt, 305
Cassoulet, 42–45
Catalonia, 207
Catherine de Médicis, 44
Caviar, 117–21
Certificates, 8, 123
Chairs, 2, 147–50
Charlemagne, Emperor, 63
Charles, Duke of Orléans, 113
Charles the Bald, King, 207
Chaucer, Geoffrey, 116
Chewing gum, 282–86
Chicken, 234, 250
Children, 4, 8, 9, 11, 28, 33–35, 50, 59, 70,
    75, 94, 105, 123, 133, 152, 154, 158, 172,
    175, 200, 204, 210, 214, 237, 244, 248,
    249, 264, 268, 275, 278, 279, 288
Chimney stack, 32, 157, 158; see also Fireplaces
Chinese, 28, 38, 88, 108, 150
Chins, 62, 63, 64–65, 282
Chocolate, 114, 115, 214
Christianity, 7, 34, 108–9, 112–13, 157, 178,
    203, 204, 213, 214, 254, 261, 293, 295;
    Catholics and Protestants, 203–4
Christkindl, 204–5
Christmas, 29, 32–36, 108, 143, 157–58,
    159, 202–6, 214, 147–51, 295
Christmas cards, 108, 113, 158
Christmas crib, 34, 203, 204
Christmas pudding, see also Pudding
Christmas trees, 202–6
Cider, 178. Cider vinegar, 223
"Cinderella," 198–99
Cities, 93–94, 107, 188, 194, 203, 214, 252,
    262, 265, 269, 273, 274; see also "Country"
Citrus fruit, 223; Grapefruit, 68
Claudius, Emperor, 198
Cleanliness, 32, 137–41, 167, 209–10, 244,
    284; see also Smelly
Clement VII, Pope, 44
Clergy, 8, 53–54, 122, 173
Clocks, 107, 109, 158
Clothes, 2, 3, 4, 7, 8, 19, 22–23, 26–27, 32, 45,
    89, 95, 96, 99, 149–50, 154–55, 172–76,
    192–96, 203, 207–10, 242–46, 295; see also
    Costumes, Sports, Shoes, Hats, Gloves
Clowns, 94, 148
Coffee, 2, 8, 9
Colonialism, 227–30
Colours, 9, 16–19, 22, 23, 88–89, 192–96,
    237–41, 292;
    faded, dull, dark, 22, 193, 194, 195, 210;
    bright, 23, 193, 198, 208–9, 234;
    coloured line, 95; see also names of indi-
    vidual colours.

Columbus, Christopher, 27, 198
Communists, 64, 79, 143, 294
Competition, 85, see also Contests
Computers, 24, 85, 175
Confetti, 7, 132
Conformity, 192, 193, 195, 207, 289; see
    also Costumes
Consumption, 260; conspicuous, 22, 34
Contests, 144, 153, 273
Control, 23–24, 72–73, 137, 147, 148,
    162–66, 179–80, 207–8, 209–10, 233,
    244, 262–65, 269, 282
Conversation, 2, 263–64; Conversational
    language, 60, 217–21
Convicts, 208
Cooking, 11, 12, 14, 23, 42–46, 49, 157,
    230, 232–33, 234, 247–50, 268, 278,
    302–4; Cooking pots, 302
Copts, 173
Corn, 70, 198, 222, 268, 283
Corsets, 17
Cossacks, 272
Costumes, Uniforms, 2, 3, 4, 7, 8, 19, 32, 45,
    73, 94, 95, 96, 123, 132, 154–55, 192, 200,
    203–4, 207–8, 295; see also Swimsuits.
"Country" opposed to "Town," 199, 269
Courage, 13, 153, 254
Crossword puzzles, 142–46
Crowd, 93–96, 99, 100–1, 102, 105, 200,
    272, 274
Cucumbers, 198
Currants, 248
Curtsying, 58–59
Custard, 235

D
Dancing, 40, 100, 108, 272, 273, 274; see
    also Tap–dancing
Darwin, Charles, 51
Dead, remembrance of the, 157, 159, 197,
    199, 200, 278; see also Funerals
Deference, 58–60, 148
Defoe, Daniel, 87–88, 92
Della Casa, Giovanni, 163, 166
Denim, 22, 192
Deprecation, 218
Deskilling, 23
Dessert, 68, 133, 189, 229, 232–34
Dickens, Charles, 172, 176, 249, 251
Dieting, 255, 257, 258, 259
Dining-room, 228, 229, 230; see also Tables
Dionysiac experience, 94, 95
Dionysius of Halicarnassus, 116
Dipping food in sauce, 69–70
Disguise, 34, 94–96, 199, 204, 263
Doctors, 8, 73, 122, 123, 255, 260
Dream analysis, 279
Drum majorettes, 94, 95–96
Dutch, 162–63

E

Easter, 213–14
Easter bunny, 212–16
Egalitarianism, 70, 128, 193, 195
Eggplant, 23
Eggs, 28, 143, 212, 213, 214, 232;
    Fish eggs, 118–21
Egyptians, ancient, 63, 88, 168, 253, 278, 303
Elasticity, 152–53, 173, 184–85, 244
Eliade, Mircea, 10
Elias, Norbert, 166
Embarrassment, 47–51, 98–106, 114, 169, 265, 293
Engels, Friedrich, 64
Engineers, 122, 123
Erasmus, Desiderius, 163, 166, 264, 266
Eskimos, see also Inuit
"Ethnic" cuisine, 11, 27, 42–46, 68, 118–20, 132–35, 178, 189, 223, 225, 247–51, 304
Etymology, see also Names, Naming
Eucharist, 7
Europeans, 2, 27, 28, 29, 64, 110, 128–29, 137, 147, 173, 178, 183, 193, 194, 198, 203, 212, 213, 223, 227–29, 242–43, 262, 272–73, 277
Examinations, 8, 123
Extensions, 168
Extinction of animal species, 28, 117–21
Eyes, 4, 84, 264, 268;
    Turkeys', 27;
    Eating, 12, 14;
    Raising eyebrows, 264;
    Winking, 264

F

Faces, recognizing, remembering, 130, 287–91;
    "Face," 49, 288;
    Facial expression, 3–4, 48, 49, 50, 199–200, 262–66, 288, 293;
    Pulling faces, 264
Factory farming, 29, 269
Family, 113, 115, 157–58, 160, 175, 199, 214, 249–50
Farewells, 59
Fascists, 79
Fashion, clothing, 22–24, 37–40, 89–90, 153, 154–55, 168–70, 175, 182–85, 192–95, 209, 242–45
Fast food, 23–24
Fasting, 257–61
Fat, 12, 29, 45, 68, 232, 247, 250
Fava beans, 44, 277–81
Feast days, Festivals, 78, 79, 80, 108, 112–15, 199–200, 202, 203, 204, 213, 247, 249–50, 259, 295; see also Christmas, Easter, Vacations, Thanksgiving, Hallowe'en
February, 112–15
Feet, 37–41, 59, 98, 138, 149, 163, 183,

272, 282; Foot-binding, 38
Ferguson, Charles, 60
Fertility, 7, 29, 33, 112, 114, 132, 199, 202, 213, 214, 295
Fidgeting, 98, 263, 282
Fin de siècle, 238
Fingernails, 39, 74, 282
Finnish, 83
Fire symbolism, 157, 158–59, 249, 293, 294, 295; see also Light
Fireplace, 5, 157–61, 205; see also Chimney stack
Fish, Fishing, 117–21, 232, 233, 234
Fitness training, 18, 23, 24, 79, 178–79, 209, 210, 255, 275
Fitzgerald, F. Scott, 18
Flags, 96, 207
Flatulence, 101, 278
Flight attendants, 1–5
Flowers, 2, 95, 133, 134, 193, 294
Flying, 1–5, 32
Fraser, John, 104, 106
Frazer, James George, 116
French, 7, 12, 14, 18, 27, 28, 29, 37, 42–46, 59, 64, 77, 100, 102, 109, 113, 119, 128, 170, 177, 190, 193, 198–99, 223, 227, 233, 238, 247, 248, 255, 303, 304–5
Freud, Sigmund, 54, 282
Fruit, 248, 294; see also individual fruits
Funerals, 96, 154
Furniture, 227–30

G

Gaelic, 83
Gaskell, Mrs. Elizabeth Cleghorn, 248, 251
Geese, 29, 43, 45
Gelatin, 232–35
Germans, 79, 100, 109, 113, 152, 170, 174, 193–94, 202–3, 204
Gestures, 57–61, 62, 64, 90, 96, 128;
    Gesticulating, 57, 262
Gide, André, 18, 20
Gift-giving, 33–34, 36, 73, 94, 113–15, 153–54, 204, 205, 214, 243
Ginseng, 28
Gloves, 2, 152–56, 183
Gooseberries, 223
Gourds, 198
Gourmets, 11, 14, 23, 118–20, 223, 224–25, 278
Grapes, 223, 293
Greeks, ancient, 12, 17, 63, 84, 129, 138–39, 159–60, 163, 253–54, 255, 263, 278–79, 304
Greeks, modern, 174, 248
Green, Greenery, 158, 202–3, 251, 269
Greetings, 57–61; see also Christmas cards, Valentines.
Guatemalans, 283

H

Habitat, depletion of, 28, 120
Haggis, 248
Hair, 3, 32, 140, 167, 168, 169–70, 207;
 Haircut, 9, 167;
 Hairdressers, 72
Hallowe'en, 197–200
Hands, 3, 17, 98, 102, 127–31, 140, 152–56;
 see also Gestures, Shaking hands,
 Fingernails
Hanway, Jonas, 87–88, 92
Hares, 212–14
Hartshorn, 232–33
Harvest, 199
Harvey, William, 254–55
Hats, 3, 17, 32, 59, 60, 89, 123, 138, 167,
 173, 183, 295;
 Caps, 168;
 Veils, 135, 295
Heads, 59, 138, 167, 168, 172, 197, 199,
 253, 264, 268, 272, 278; see also Hats.
Health, 9, 16–20, 60, 137–39, 162–63, 164,
 167, 178–79, 209, 257
Hearth, 228, 248; see also Fireplaces
Hearts, 114, 127, 128, 129, 252–56, 266,
 294; eating, 11, 13, 255;
 Heart attacks, 255
Heating, 139, 157, 230
Hebrew, 196, 294
Heraldry, 208, 294
Herodotus, 166
Hinduism, 108
Hitchcock, Alfred, 37
Hockney, David, 240
Holidays, see also Feast days, Vacations
Holme, Randle, 168, 171
Homer, 138–39, 141, 256, 277, 281
Honeymoons, 7
Honour, 49, 59, 123, 125, 153, 155, 157,
 165, 233, 254, 288
Horace, 99, 106
Houses, 149, 157–60, 200, 230, 267–68,
 299–300
Howlers, 190
Hunting, 28, 77, 254, 268, 269–70, 297
Huxley, Aldous, 18
Huxley, Julian 53
Huysmans, Joris-Karl, 238

I

Ice, 298
Ice cream, 209
Impropriety, 47–51, 98–105, 147–48, 162–65,
 217, 219, 263–65, 284–85, 289
Indians, 88, 108, 193
Indians, American, 26, 27, 28, 44, 67–68,
 70, 174, 199, 227, 259, 261, 283, 297,
 301
Indigo, 193–94, 195

Indoors, 16–17, 158, 203–4, 214
Informality, 18, 22, 69–70, 193, 195, 230,
 274; see also Conversational language
Initiations, 6–10, 14, 19, 24, 34–35, 62–63,
 119, 123, 124, 132, 135, 140, 194, 200,
 213, 244, 258, 285
Inuit, 297–301
Iranians, 27, 118, 163
Irish, 109, 153, 272
Isinglass, 232
Islam, 259, 261
Israelis, 70
Italians, 27, 38, 42, 44, 79, 89, 128, 278, 302

J

Jamaicans, 70; see also Caribbean
Japanese, 27, 115, 148, 149, 252, 284
Jeans, 22, 192–96
Jefferson, Thomas, 178
Jelly, Jello, 232–36;
 Jelly-moulds, 233–34
Jesus Christ, 204, 213, 254, 258, 293
Jewellery, 203, 253
Johnson, Samuel, 48, 51, 83, 226
Jokes, 115, 199–200; see also Howlers
Josselyn, John, 28, 31
Joyce, James, 12, 15
Judaism, 7, 178, 261
Julian, Emperor, 63, 66

K

Kandinsky, Wassily, 240
Keeping food, 13, 69, 234
Kelly, Gene, 274
Khomeini, the Ayatollah, 64
Kidneys, 12
Kissing, 57–58
Kitchens, 23, 230;
 Kitchen tables, 228–29
Kneeling, 58
Knitting, 172–76, 184, 209
Koreans, 108
Kraft General Foods, 235
Kurds, 104

L

Labat, Jean-Baptiste, 69, 71
La Tour-Landry, Geoffroy, 255, 256
Laughing, 32–33, 105, 110, 263
Lavoisier, Antoine Laurent de, 223
Lawrence, Saint, 159
Lawyers, 8, 73, 122
Left and Right, 39, 59, 127–31, 174
Legs, 37–38, 39, 40, 96, 142, 148, 182, 183,
 184, 185, 242–45
Leisure, 22, 80, 175, 210, 269; see also
 Vacations, Work
Lemons, 223
Lenin, Nikolay, 64
Lennon, John, 64

Lent, 213, 259
Lentils, 222, 304
Lévi-Strauss, Claude, 49, 51
Librarians, 123
"Light" food, 29, 45
Light symbolism, 198, 199–200, 203, 205, 213; see also Star, Fire symbolism
"Like," 219–20
Lipstick, 9, 294
Liver, 11, 12
Lots, drawing, 279
Lucia, Saint, 205
Luck, 134, 214–15, 149, 249, 279
Luggage, 3
Lydgate, John, 233, 236

M

Machines, 78, 175, 178, 254–55
Magi, 203, 249, 250, 279
Mahogany, 227–31
Mao Tse-Tung, 150
Marriage, 113–14, 115, 128–29, 132–36, 158, 159, 160;
    Married people, 4, 33, 145; see also Weddings
Marshmallows, 234
Marx, Karl, 64
Mary, the Virgin, 194
Mathers, Edward Powys, 145
Meals, 2, 12, 22, 29, 30, 104, 129, 133–34, 163, 178, 180, 187–91, 228, 230, 233–34, 259, 260, 283, 303–4
Meat, 11–15, 27, 28, 29, 43, 44, 69, 223, 233–34, 247, 248, 250, 267–71, 302, 305; see also Gelatin
Medicine, 17, 137–38, 255, 259, 279–80; see also Doctors
Meditation, 108, 173
Melons, 198
Memory, 287–91
Men, 1, 2, 3, 4, 17, 37, 62–66, 74, 87, 112–15, 128–29, 138, 149, 150, 154, 158, 160, 163, 164, 167, 172–73, 183, 184, 185, 193, 194, 202, 203, 212, 242–43, 244, 245, 254, 275, 279
Menu, 13, 187–91
Meringer, Rudolf, 54–55, 56
Messiaen, Olivier, 240
Metaphors, 237, 252, 253, 255
Mexicans, 68, 283, 294–95
Microwave, 250
Military, 94, 95, 123, 129, 137, 172, 208, 249, 284, 304
Mind, 49, 98; see also Brain
Mittens, 152, 154
Mitterrand, François, 263
Mnemonics, 239, 289–90
Mobility, 1, 2–3, 4, 6, 23, 93–96, 185, 193, 209, 250
Modesty, 16–17, 154, 183–84

Monasteries, 108–9
Money, Rich people, 1, 9, 14, 16, 17, 18, 21–24, 73, 74, 80, 122, 124–25, 153–54, 169, 188, 193, 227, 228, 230, 243, 248–49, 260
Montagné, Prosper, 43, 46
Moon, 213; The Man in the Moon, 213
Moore, Clement C., 32, 36
Mother of Vinegar, 224
Movies, 37, 110, 149
Murphy, Gerald and Sara, 18
Mussolini, Benito, 79

N

Nabokov, Vladimir, 237, 241
Nakedness, 16–17, 18, 99, 182, 183, 184. Bare head, 59; bare feet, 59, 183; bare hands, 154, 155; bared legs, 243
Names, naming, 4, 7, 8, 13, 27, 70, 109, 128, 142, 150, 157, 175, 189, 197, 213, 223, 227, 233, 247, 254, 257, 268, 274, 284, 294–95, 297–301, 303;
    proper names, 52, 107–8, 150, 175, 179, 204–5, 212, 213, 234;
    remembering names, 287–91
Nazis, 79, 110, 143
Newpapers, 144, 145
New Year, 33
Nicholas, Saint, 36, 203, 204
Noise, 96, 107–8, 273, 284–85
Nomenclator, 287–88
Non-conformity, 64, 65, 192–93, 208
Nose-picking, 101, 282
Nurses, 3
Nylon, 242, 243

O

O'Connor, Donald, 274
Offal, 11–15
Olives, 68
Olympic Games, 159
Opposites, System of, 17, 128
Orange, 188, 197, 198, 200
Outdoors, 16–17, 93–96, 203–4, 214
Overalls, 193
Ovid, 116
Oxygen, 223–24
Ozu, Yasujiro, 149

P

Pantihose, 244, 245
Pants, 4, 23, 40, 150, 183; see also Jeans
Papua New Guinea, 167–68
Parades, 93–97
Parasols, 17, 88–89, 89–90, 209; see also Umbrellas
Parents, 8, 34–35, 59, 129, 237, 241, 278
Parks, 269
Parties, 33, 100, 134, 229, 233, 235
Pasta, 304

Patriotism, 94, 95, 175, 176, 199, 249
Peacocks, 26, 27, 29
Peppermint, 284
Pepys, Samuel, 249, 251
Perfume, 153, 203
Perry, Matthew Calbraith, 148, 151
Peruvians, 77, 174
Pesto, 42
Pests, 267, 269–70; see also Vermin
Petrossian, Melkom and Mougcheg, 119
Pets, 269
Phallic symbols, 33, 135, 198, 295
Pharmacists, 123
Phoenicians, 212–13
Photographs, 135, 157, 158, 188
Pickling, Pickles, 223, 224
Pies, 199; Mince-pies, 251
Pigeons, 268
Pilots, 1, 3, 4
Pink, 194, 292
Plath, Sylvia, 11
Plato, 256
Pliny the Elder, 255
Politeness, 57–61, 217–21, 262–65, 285
Politics, 78, 96; see also Revolutionaries
Pollution, 24, 120, 178; Ritual pollution, 128, 129, 164, 165, 279
Pop drinks, 23, 179
Porridge, 247, 248, 303, 304
Port, 229
Porters, 75
Portuguese, 64, 87–88, 108, 174
Post, Emily, 5
Postal service, 113; Postmen, 72
Powell, Eleanor, 274
Prato, the Merchant of, 233
Praying, 58, 60, 63–64, 107, 108, 258
Pregnancy, 33, 100, 177–78, 197, 198, 278
Private and Public, 93–96, 140, 168, 199–200, 203, 205, 228, 262, 263, 264–65
Processions, 94–95, 96
Productivity, 22
Professionals, 8, 73, 74, 122–26
Professors, 8, 52–53, 54, 60, 104, 122, 123, 207, 289
Promiscuity, 1
Propaganda, 143
Prophets, 64
Protests, 96, 163, 192–93, 258
Prunes, 248
Psychologists, Psychiatrists, 122, 238
Pudding, 247;
    Plum or Christmas, 133, 247–52;
    Pudding-cloth, 248, 249, 251
Pumpkins, 197–201
Puritanical attitudes, 96, 138–39, 178, 180, 194–95
Purity, 1, 7, 112, 140, 159–60, 163, 203, 204; see also White

Purple, 193, 294
Pythagoras, Pythagoreans, 278, 279, 280, 281

Q
Questions, asking, 217–18, 219

R
Rabbits, 212, 213, 268, 269
Racism, 3, 208, 273
Raffald, Elizabeth, 236
Railways, 1, 2, 43, 165, 229–30
Ramadan, 259
Reading, 288; Reading silently, 84
Recipes, 45, 70, 134, 189, 199, 232–33, 249–50, 268
Red, 32, 33, 47–50, 95, 98, 202, 204, 209, 228, 252, 292–96
Refrigeration, 69, 118, 233, 234
Religion, 7, 34, 78, 80, 96, 108–9, 140, 159–60, 214, 258–59; see also Christianity, Judaism, Islam, Hinduism
Restaurants, 24, 89, 165, 187–90, 304–5; see also Waiters
Retirement, 80
Revolutionaries, 64, 172, 176, 294; French Revolution, 40, 172, 176, 208; American Revolution, 208
Riches, see also Money
Riddles, 47, 114, 142–46
Right, see also Left and Right
Rimbaud, Arthur, 238, 241
Rimsky-Korsakov, Nikolay Andreievich, 240
Rings, 7, 114, 123, 128–29, 132, 249
Rituals, 6, 7, 8, 9, 12, 18–19, 57–60, 93–96, 108, 112, 123, 132–36, 138, 140, 153, 154, 159–60, 203, 204–5
Riviera, French, 18
Romans, ancient, 17, 48, 77, 84, 119, 129, 158, 159, 163, 198, 212, 255, 287–88
Rombauer, Irma S., 234, 236, 271
Royalty, 63, 94, 119, 148, 153, 193, 207, 249, 263, 279
Russians, 109–10, 118–20
Rustic image, 188–89, 199
Rutt, Richard, 173, 175, 176, 186, 246

S
Sailors, 172, 209
Salt, 222, 248
Saluting, 59, 60
Santa Claus, 32–36, 94, 95, 158, 202–5, 214, 295
Sanskrit, 294
Saturnalia, 249
Sauerkraut, 223
Sausages, 43, 45, 247, 248
Scandinavians, 205, 230
Scriabin, Aleksandr Nikolayevich, 240
Sea symbolism, 194, 209
Seaside, 16–20, 209

Secretaries, 60
Self-consciousness, 49–50, 57, 98–106
Self-sufficiency, 72
Seneca, Lucius Annaeus, 198, 201
Serbo-Croatian, 83
Service charge, 73–74
Sewing, 174, 209, 232
Sex, 19, 28, 29, 37, 47, 133, 135, 158, 160, 167–68, 198, 242, 243, 244–45, 259–60, 284, 294, 295
Sexism, 1–5, 17, 37–40, 49, 58, 63, 74, 128–29, 148, 194, 242, 245
Shakespeare, William, 13, 15, 119, 121
Shaking hands, 57, 59, 129, 153, 154
Shampoo, 140, 168
Sharing food, drink, 12, 134, 178
Shaving, 62, 63, 65, 168
Shaw, George Bernard, 82
Ships, 1, 2, 228
Shish kebabs, 12
Shoes, 30, 37–41, 149, 152, 153, 183, 242, 272–74; see also Boots, Sneakers
Shopping, 24, 34, 250, 268; Shopkeepers, 78
Showers, 137–41
Shrugging, 57, 145, 262
Silk, 243
Singles, 3, 33, 115
Sitting, 147–50
Skin, 16–19
Skirts, 183–84, 204, 242, 243; Miniskirts, 149–50, 244
Sky symbolism, 194
Slime, 163–64, 284
Smelly, being, 101, 140, 259
Smiling, 3, 98, 264
Smoking, 9, 32–33, 95, 145, 177, 180, 284
Sneakers, 22, 24, 209
Snobbery, see also Status
Snow, 297–301
Socks, 173
Solidarity, group, 6–9, 123–25, 193, 259
Sorrel, 223
Soup, 2, 247, 248, 302–6
Sourness, 222–26
Souvenirs, 19
Spanish, 27, 29, 44, 70, 89, 95, 99–100, 108, 207, 212, 227, 272, 293; Armada, 228
Sparrows, 268
Specialization, 148–49, 155
Speech, 52–56, 83, 84–85, 130, 142, 217–21, 288; see also Names
Speed whiskers, 209
Spelling of English, 82–86
Spirits, distilled, 178
Spitting, 162–66
Spooner, William Archibald, 52–56; Spoonerisms, 52–56

Sports, 124, 155, 209, 268; Sports clothes, 23, 155, 209; see Olympic Games, Baseball
Squashes, 197–98, 199
Squirrels, 267–71
Standardization, 179
Star, 204
Status, 1–4, 6–9, 12, 13–14, 17, 18–19, 21–24, 37–38, 40, 48, 58, 63, 65, 74–75, 88–89, 120, 122–26, 128, 148, 149, 152–55, 167, 173, 188, 189–90, 194, 228, 229, 230, 243, 262–65, 275; see also Gourmets, Upper class
Stew, 44, 268
Stillness, 148, 262–65
Stockings, 9, 33, 149, 158, 173, 183, 242–46
Stripes, 207–11
Structuralism, 49
Sturgeon, 117–21
Sugar, 69, 229–30, 248, 283
Suits, business, 24
Sultanas, 248
Sun, 213; Sunday, 213
Sunglasses, 19
Suntan, 9, 16–20, 90, 184; Suntan lotion, 17, 19
Surgeons, 73, 172–73
Suspender-belts, 244–45
Swearing, 7, 45, 62, 64, 160
Sweaters, 22, 175, 184, 209
Sweetbreads, 14
Sweetness, 222, 248, 250
Swimming, 16, 18
Swimsuits, 17, 19, 38, 175, 209
Synaesthesia, 237–41

T
Table manners, 129, 134–35, 154, 162–63, 164, 187–88, 229, 304
Table settings, 2, 118, 133–35, 228, 229, 233–34
Tables, dining-room, 227–30
Taboos, food, 11–14, 267–71, 278–79, 281
Tails, 11, 26, 268
Tap-dancing, 272–76
Tattoos, 9, 252
Taxation, 63
Taxi drivers, 75, 76, 88
Tea, 2, 8
Teachers, 73, 123
Tears, 164, 263, 264
Telephones, 107–8, 119, 290
Television, 94, 101, 107, 195, 274
Thanksgiving, 26–31, 199
Thinness, 9, 179, 185, 188, 208, 234, 250
Time, 6, 22, 73, 90, 107, 108–9, 124, 134, 139, 143–44, 179, 188, 247, 249–50, 289
Tipping, 72–76

Tomato ketchup, 224
Tongues, human, 222, 264
Toothpaste, 210
Toothpicks, 283
Tourism, 18–19, 42–45, 75, 79;
    Tour guides, 72, 75; see also Travel,
    Vacations
Toynbee, A.J., 53
Toys, 32–33
Traffic, see also Cars
Travel, 1–5, 7, 18, 22, 102, 143, 298, 299
Trousers, see also Pants
T-Shirts, 22, 189
Turkeys, 26–31
Turks, 27, 174, 248
Turnips, 44

U

Umbrellas, 87–92; see also Parasols
Underwear, 173, 175, 182–83, 184, 294; see
    also Suspender-belts
Uniforms, see also Costumes
Unknown soldier, 159
Upper class, 17, 18, 21–22, 37, 38, 40, 58, 63,
    75, 85, 89, 90, 119, 122, 152–54, 169,
    174–75, 184, 194, 263, 273
Uruguayans, 305

V

Vacations, 7, 16–20, 77–81, 209, 259; see
    also Tourism, Travel
Valentines, St Valentine's Day, 112–15,
    154, 252
Valeriano, Pietro, 44
Van Gennep, Arnold, 10
Vanier, Jean, 104
Veblen, Thorstein, 21–22, 25
Vegetarianism, 278
Verjuice, 223
Vermin, 63, 169, 225, 268
Vianney, Jean-Baptiste, Saint, Curé d'Ars,
    173
Vinegar, 12, 222–26, 233
Virginity, 159–60
Visions, 6, 259

W

Wait, Paul and Pearl, 234
Waiters, 2, 74, 75, 76, 119, 154, 189, 190
Waiting, 124, 143–44
Walking, 4, 24, 273; Walking-sticks, 89
Washing, see also Cleanliness
Waste, 21–22, 200, 229–30, 245
Watches, 107, 109, 253
Water, 120, 133, 137–41, 178, 182–86, 300,
    304; Mineral water, 179; see also Swimming,
    Sea symbolism
Waving, 59–60
Wealth, see also Money
Webster, Noah, 83

Weddings, 7, 132–35, 154, 194, 295;
    Wedding cakes, 132–35
Weight, body, 3
White, 32, 115, 133, 135, 154, 169, 204,
    209, 210, 292, 293, 295; skin, 17, 19, 90,
    153
Wigs, 123, 167–71
Wilde, Oscar, 21, 22, 25
Wilfred the Hairy, Count, 207
Wilgefortis, Saint, 64
Wine, 177–81, 223, 224, 225, 278, 293,
    303, 304
Woad, 193
Women, 1–5, 17, 33, 37–40, 49, 58, 63–64,
    74, 87, 89–90, 95–96, 100, 104, 112–15,
    128–29, 130, 132, 134–35, 138, 139,
    148, 149, 154, 155, 158–60, 163, 164,
    167–68, 172, 173, 177–78, 182–85, 193,
    194, 202–3, 240, 242–45, 274, 284
Wood, 227–31, 283
Wool, 172–76, 184, 243, 295
Work, Workers, 17, 18, 22, 23, 24, 77–81,
    124, 125, 153–54, 169–70, 172, 192–93,
    210, 259, 284, 288; Not Working,
    21–22, 37, 38, 40, 77–81, 90, 153, 209,
    210, 269
Worry-beads, 283
Writing, 84, 142–46, 187, 188
Wynne, Arthur, 143

X

Xenophon, 166

Y

Yeast, 303
Yellow, 29, 207, 293
Yule log, 159, 204

Z

Zambia, 68
Zuppa inglese, 302